Michelle Stewart

S. MARY
GEOGRAP

CW01143733

31

Investigati[g] Geography A

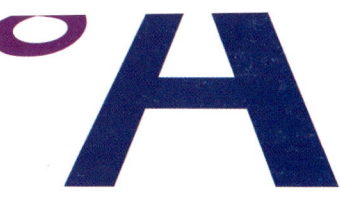

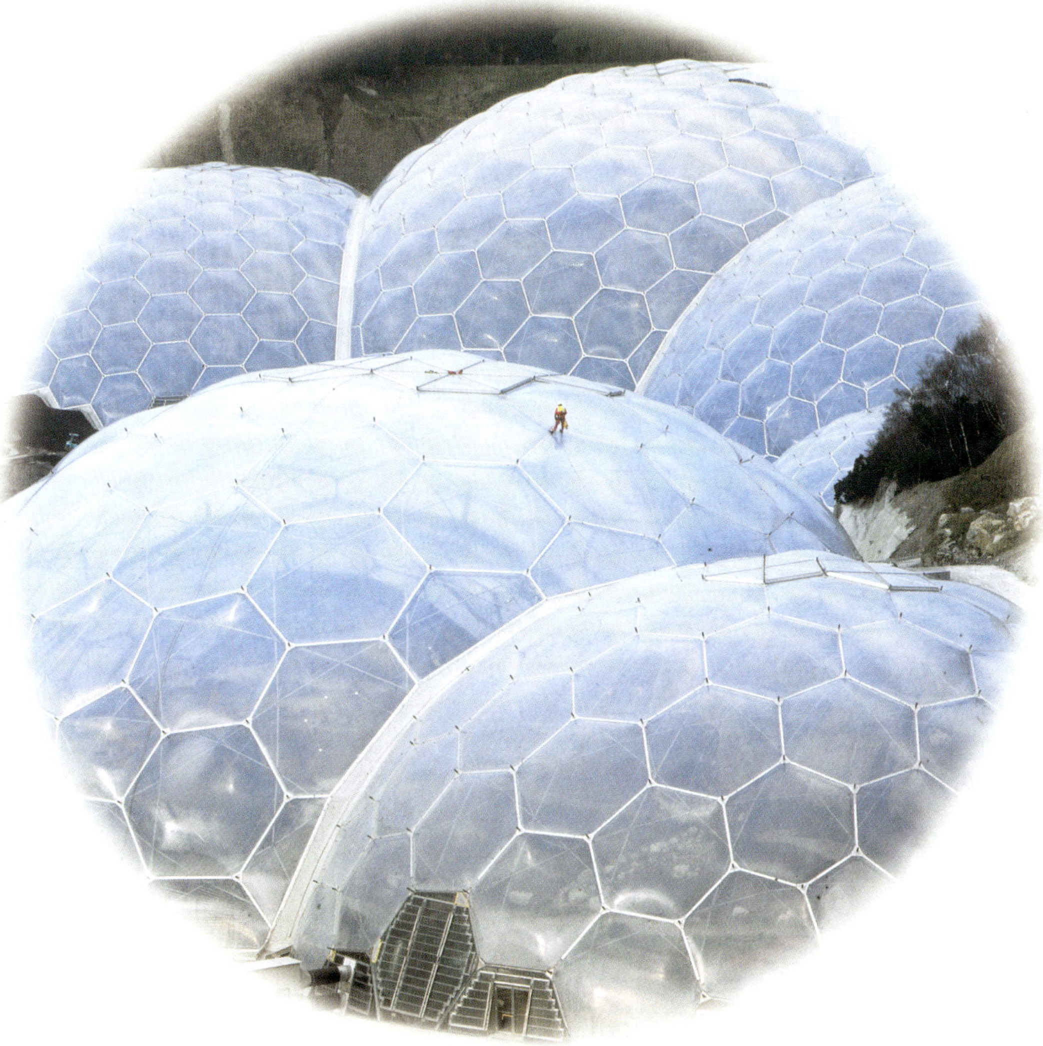

JACKIE ARUNDALE · SUE BERMINGHAM · SIMON CHANDLER · CHRIS DURBIN
GREG HART · BOB JONES · LINDA KING · FRED MARTIN · DIANE SWIFT
SERIES EDITORS: KEITH GRIMWADE & CHRIS DURBIN

Hodder & Stoughton
A MEMBER OF THE HODDER HEADLINE GROUP

Acknowledgements

The front cover illustration shows the Eden Project, Cornwall; reproduced courtesy of © Herbie Knott.

The publishers would like to thank the following individuals, institutions and companies for permission to reproduce copyright illustrations in this book(numbers given are figure numbers): Action Plus, 3.7bl; © Adrian Fisk, 4.1, 4.2; AFP Photos, 4.19; Alaska Wilderness League, 1.30; Andrew Ward/Life File, 1.23, 3.7cl, 6.2cl, 6.13cl; AP, 4.4, 6.27, 6.34; © Ashanti Goldfields, 2.2, 2.6, 2.25, 2.26, 2.38; © B & C Alexander, 3.4 (1); B & C Alexander/© Ann Hawthorne, 3.4 (2); © Bettmann/Corbis, 6.25; Lodestone Publishing, 1.8, 3.3; Cape Grim B.A.P.S./Simon Fraser/Science Photo Library, 3.8 (1), 3.8 (5); © Casio, 1.1; © Charles O'Rear/Corbis, 6.5tl; Cliff Threadgold, 6.2br; Corporate Communications Unit, Stoke-on-Trent City Council, 2.20, 2.21; © Craig Aurness/Corbis, 1.25; Digital Stock, p4r; Digital Vision, p28bg; Emma Lee/Life File, 1.22, 3.7tl, 3.7tr, 6.13l; Eyewire, p30 (flags), p94bg; Françoise Sauze/Science Photo Library, 3.8 (2); © Fred Martin, 1.12, 1.26, 1.27, 1.28, 1.34; GE Astro Space/Science Photo Library, 1.3, 1.4; GeoInformation Group, 1.9; Gladstone Museum, Longton, 2.12; Graham Burns/Life File, 6.2tl; © Greg Hart, 4.5, 4.17; Ikon Imaging, p54bg; Ingram Publishing, p6r, 1.32, p30bg, p54bg, p57 (camera, toothbrush); Jeremy Hoare/Life File, 1.10, 6.1tr, 6.1bl, 6.13cr; Jerry Mason/Science Photo Library, 3.8 (6); Jon Woodhouse/Life File, 5.9; Kent News, 6.19r; Landeshauptstadt, Dresden, 2.32; Lionel Moss/Life File, 5.7, 6.2cr; © Mark Edwards/Still Pictures, 6.17; © Crown Copyright, The Met Office, p49tr, 3.10, 3.14; © Michael Busselle/Corbis, 5.27; Mike Arundale, 4.14, 4.21, 4.28, 4.29, 4.30, 5.1, 5.2, 5.3, 5.4, 5.5, 5.13, 5.20; Mike Maidment/Life File, 6.19l; Nicole Sutton/Life File, 3.4 (5); Nigel Shuttleworth/Life File, 6.2tr; PA Photos/EPA, 1.20; © Paul Seheult, Eye Ubiquitous/Corbis, 3.8 (4); Peter Dunkley/Life File, 1.24; Peter Harkin/Life File, 6.1tl; Photoair, 4.25; Photodisc, p4bg, 1.2, p5bl, p7bg, p10b, p12bg, 1.19, 1.33, p44bg, p45r, p45b, p46bg, p48bg, 3.9, p50bg, p52br, p54tl, p54bg, p56bg, p57 (sunglasses, penknife, cars, umbrella) p59br, p60bg, p68bg, p70bg, 4.16, p76bg, 4.22, p86bg, 5.10bg, 5.11bg, p92tr, p93r, p100bg, 5.29, 5.31, p103bg, 6.1br, 6.3, 6.4, 6.5, 6.13r, p113r, 6.35; Richard Powers/Life File, 3.4 (4), 3.22, 6.2bl; © Robert Estall/Corbis, 5.26; © Roger Ressmeyer/Corbis, 5.28; Shell Nigeria Images, 6.32; © Starke Foto Dokument 01099 Dresden, 2.3, 2.4, 2.5, 2.7, 2.9, 2.29, 2.30; Stephen Kraseman/Science Photo Library, 3.8 (3); Sue Cunningham/SCP, 3.4 (2); © Tom Bean/Corbis, 1.29; Tony Craddock/Science Photo Library, 1.17; © US National Park Service, 5.21; Werner Forman Archive/British Museum, 2.10; © Yann Arthus-Bertand/Corbis, 6.5bl (b = bottom; t = top; l = left; r = right; c = centre; bg = background)

The publishers would also like to thank the following for permission to reproduce material in this book: © Bill Bryson. Extracted from Made in America by Bill Bryson, published by Black Swan, a division of Transworld Publishers. All rights reserved; © The Guardian for extracts from 'Grim find of 58 bodies …' by Nick Hopkins, Jeevan Vasager, Paul Kelso, Andrew Osborn, Guardian, 28 March 2000; extracts from Miss Smilla's Feeling for Snow by Peter Høeg, Harvill, 1993 © Peter Høeg and Munksgaard/Rosinante, Copenhagen, 1992, English translation © Farrar, Straus & Giroux Inc. and The Harvill Press, 1993. Translated from the Danish by F. David. Reproduced by permission of The Harvill Press; extracted information on pages 50 and 52 from The Met Office (see extracts for acknowledgement); © The Observer for extracts from 'Film of the week: "'Not one less'" by Peter Preston, Observer, 25 June 2000;maps reproduced from Ordnance Survey mapping with the permission of the Controller of Her Majesty's Stationery Office, © Crown copyright, Licence No. 100019872; Trentham Books for the extract from Visions of the Future: why we need to teach for tomorrow by D. Hicks and C. Holden (eds), Trentham, 1995; "Diagnostic and Formative Assessment of Student Learning" article by David Leat and Julie McGrane, pages 4-7, January 2000 edition of Teaching Geography.

Every effort has been made to trace and acknowledge ownership of copyright. The publishers will be glad to make suitable arrangements with any copyright holders whom it has not been possible to contact.

Note about the Internet links in the book. The user should be aware that URLs or web addresses change regularly. Every effort has been made to ensure the accuracy of the URLs provided in this book on going to press. It is inevitable, however, that some will change. It is sometimes possible to find a relocated web page, by just typing in the address of the home page for a websie in the URL window of your browser.

Orders: please contact Bookpoint Ltd, 130 Milton Park, Abingdon, Oxon OX14 4SB. Telephone: (44) 01235 827720. Fax: (44) 01235 400454. Lines are open from 9.00 - 6.00, Monday to Saturday, with a 24 hour message answering service. Email address: orders@bookpoint.co.uk

British Library Cataloguing in Publication Data
A catalogue record for this title is available from the British Library

ISBN 0 340 80375 4

First Published 2002
Impression number   10 9 8 7 6 5 4 3 2
Year   2007 2006 2005 2004 2003

Copyright in all editorial matters © 2002 Keith Grimwade and Chris Durbin
Copyright © 2002 Jackie Arundale, Susan Bermingham, Simon Chandler, Greg Hart, Linda King, Fred Martin and Diane Swift.

All rights reserved. This work is copyright. Permission is given for copies to be made of pages provided they are used exclusively within the institution for which this work has been purchased. For reproduction for any other purpose, permission must first be obtained in writing from the publishers.

Designed and typeset by Nomad Graphique
Printed in Italy for Hodder & Stoughton Educational, a division of Hodder Headline Plc, 338 Euston Road, London NW1 3BH.

Investigating Geography A

Contents

1	Connecting Places	4
2	Development: Change in Contrasting Localities	24
3	Weather and Climate	44
4	Economic Activity	64
5	National Parks	84
6	Population	104
	Glossary	124
	Index	130

1 Connecting places

Where am I?

Am I at the right place?

You can see the day, date and time on the wristwatch. But look again. It also tells you where you are. The display gives figures for your **latitude** and **longitude**. This tells you where you are on any place on earth (see pages 12 and 13).

There are far more figures here than you usually see for the latitude and longitude of a place in the index of an atlas. This is because the measurements are exact to within a few metres. The wristwatch will also tell you the height of the land you are on.

△ **Figure 1.1** The Casio Global Positioning wristwatch.

The Global Positioning System

The watch uses technology called the **Global Positioning System** (GPS). Aircraft and ships have been using the GPS to find their way for many years. Now the technology is available for everyone.

△ **Figure 1.2** Most ships and aircraft now use the Global Positioning System for navigation

Activities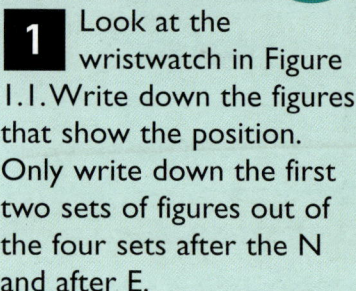

1 Look at the wristwatch in Figure 1.1. Write down the figures that show the position. Only write down the first two sets of figures out of the four sets after the N and after E.

2 If you already know how to find places from their latitude and longitude, find the country shown by the figures. You could even find the city.

4 INVESTIGATING GEOGRAPHY A

How does it work?

The Global Positioning System uses satellites and computers to tell you where you are. The watch has a receiver that picks up data sent from satellites. These are special satellites that pinpoint places on the Earth. There are 24 of them that orbit the Earth. It needs three satellites to pinpoint where you are and another one to show your height. They are about 20 000 km above the Earth so they are much too small and far away to see.

▷ **Figure 1.3** Receivers get signals from satellites that pinpoint where they are

How satellites link people

People also use satellites to talk to each other, either by phone or by email. This is done by bouncing messages off them to places all around the Earth. Television pictures can also be bounced off satellites. Satellites are used to take pictures so that people can find out more about the Earth. News and information travels fast from place to place in today's world.

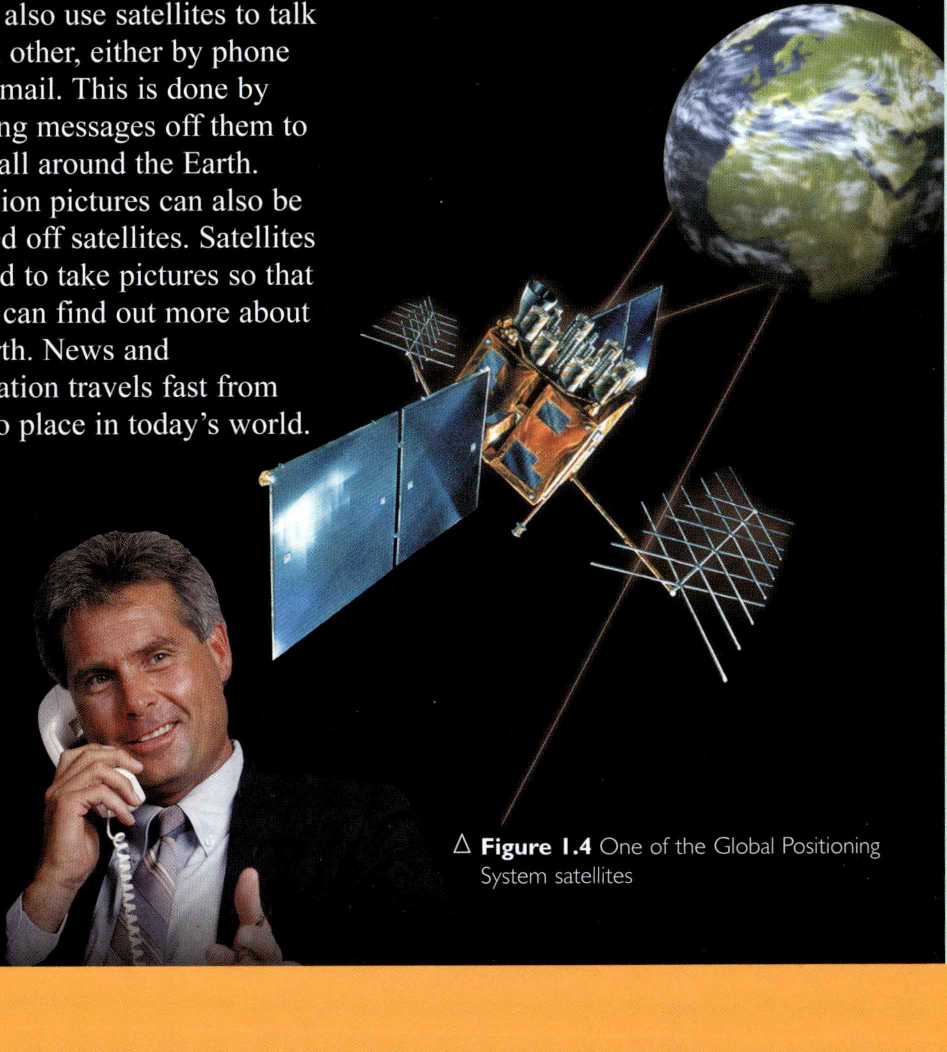

△ **Figure 1.4** One of the Global Positioning System satellites

Activities

3 Draw a diagram with labels to show how the Global Positioning System works. Include:
- at least four satellites
- the Earth
- a GPS receiver that can look like a watch
- lines to show information being sent.

4 Draw and label an advertisement to show the advantages of using the GPS system for someone who needs to know where they are. This could be for a lorry driver or for a pilot.

5 Think of some other questions you could ask about the Global Positioning System. Write them down and see if you can find the answers by using websites on the Internet.

1 Connecting Places 5

What's the number of my place?

Grids on maps

You may already have used an **Ordnance Survey** (OS) map for geography work at school. OS maps have a grid of numbers to describe where places are. You can find a grid square by using a four-figure **grid reference**. You can pinpoint a place in a square by using a six-figure grid reference. Lines from top to bottom of the map are called **Eastings**. Lines across the map are called **Northings**.

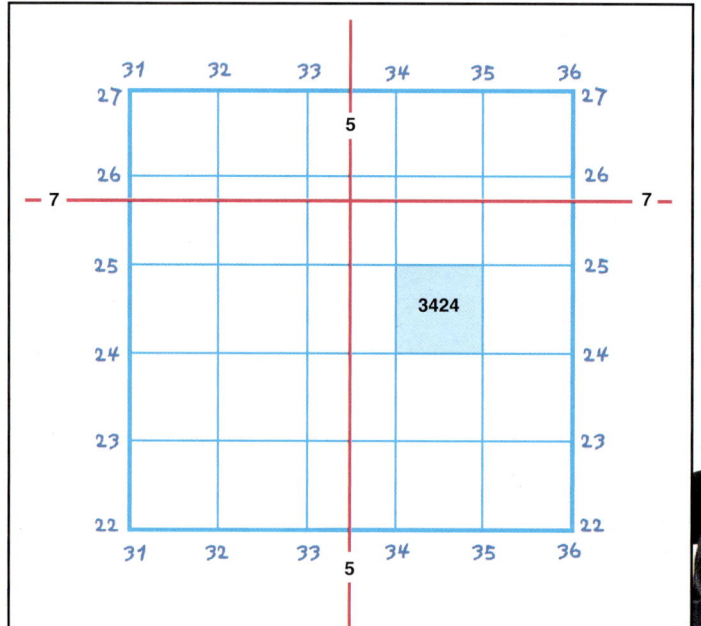

▷ **Figure 1.5** How to give a four-figure and a six-figure grid reference

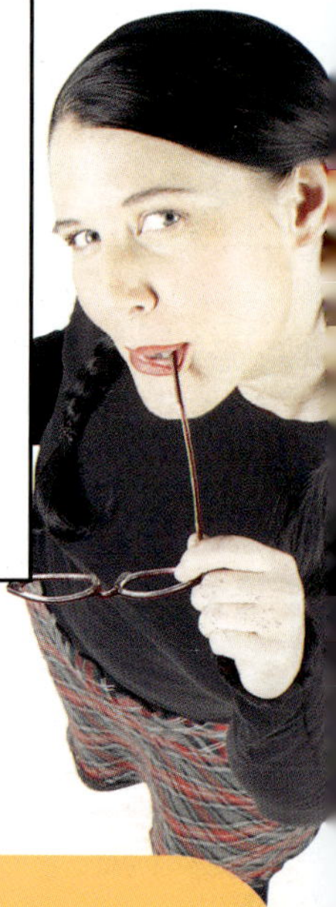

> ### Reminder – using a four-figure grid reference
>
> 1. Find the line to the left side of the square (the Easting).
> 2. Look along the top or bottom of the map to find the two figures for this line. Write down the two figures, e.g. 34.
> 3. Find the line along the bottom of the square (the Northing).
> 4. Look along the right or left side of the map to find the two figures for this line, e.g. 24. Write these two figures after the first two figures to give the four-figure grid reference for the square, e.g. 3424.

> ### Reminder – using a six-figure grid reference
>
> 1. Find the first two figures of the four-figure reference, e.g. 33.
> 2. Work out how far the point is away from the next Easting line, e.g. towards line 34. Think of it as nine invisible lines so that line 5 is half way across the square. Write the figure, e.g. 335.
> 3. Find the second set of numbers of the four-figure reference, e.g. 25.
> 4. Work out how far the point is up from the next Northing line, e.g. towards 26. Think of it as nine invisible lines across the map. A bit more than half way could be 7, e.g. at 257.
> 5. The full six-figure grid reference for the point would then be 335257.

6 INVESTIGATING GEOGRAPHY A

How big is my place?

You can measure the size of a place from a map by using the map scale. The scale is written as a figure called a **representative fraction** (RF). For example, a RF of 1:50 000 shows that one unit on the map represents 50 000 of the same units on the ground.

One way to measure size is to measure the distance between points. You can also measure or estimate the **area**. You can see some schools on a 1:50 000 scale OS map, but you will need a larger scale map to work out distance and area accurately.

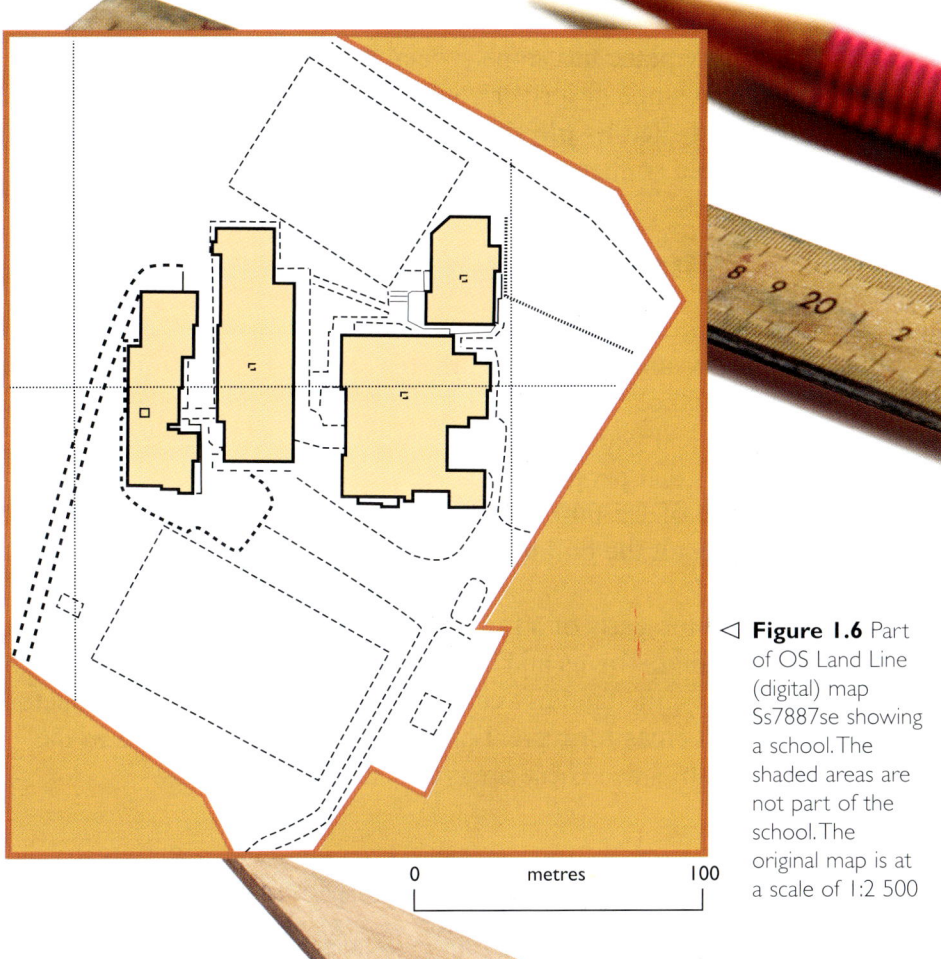

◁ **Figure 1.6** Part of OS Land Line (digital) map Ss7887se showing a school. The shaded areas are not part of the school. The original map is at a scale of 1:2 500

Reminder – calculating distance from a map's scale

A map distance of 5 cm on a ruler on a 1:50 000 scale map would be:

5 cm × 50 000 (map scale) = 250 000 cm = 2 500 metres = 2.5 km.

You can also measure distance by laying a straight edge of paper across the map. Then mark the start and finish points and see how far this is on the map's line scale.

Activities

1 Use a map of your secondary school to find the four-figure grid reference for the square it is in on an Ordnance Survey map.

2 Locate the primary schools in the area that others in your class have come from. Then measure the distances from the primary schools you have all come from to your secondary school.

3 On a map of at least 1:2 500 scale, measure the longest and the shortest distances across your secondary school. You can also work out its area. You could do this for the map in Figure 1.6.

1 Connecting Places   7

What's at my place?

What features make a place?

Every place has some special features that make them unique. A steep slope or a river could be part of its natural landscape. This is also called its **physical geography**. Houses and roads are built by people so they are part of the **human geography**.

What can you see by looking down?

Maps and **vertical air photos** show some features of a place. An Ordnance Survey (OS) 1:50 000 scale map is useful to show the physical geography and how land is used over a large area. The ways that people use the land is called the area's **land use**. At a scale of 1:5 000, a vertical air photo is usually clear enough to show all the buildings, roads, woods and fields.

In some parts of a town or city, most of the land is used for housing. Towns and cities are also called **urban** areas. In other places, the land use can be more mixed with houses, factories and open areas for recreation. The most open areas are in the countryside. These areas are called **rural** areas.

ICT activity

Use the Multimap web site to find maps of the area where you live: **www.multimap.com** If you live in a large urban area, you can also find a vertical air photo. You may be able to see your house.

Activities

1. Look at the map in Figure 1.7 is this an urban or rural area? Give evidence for your answer from the map.

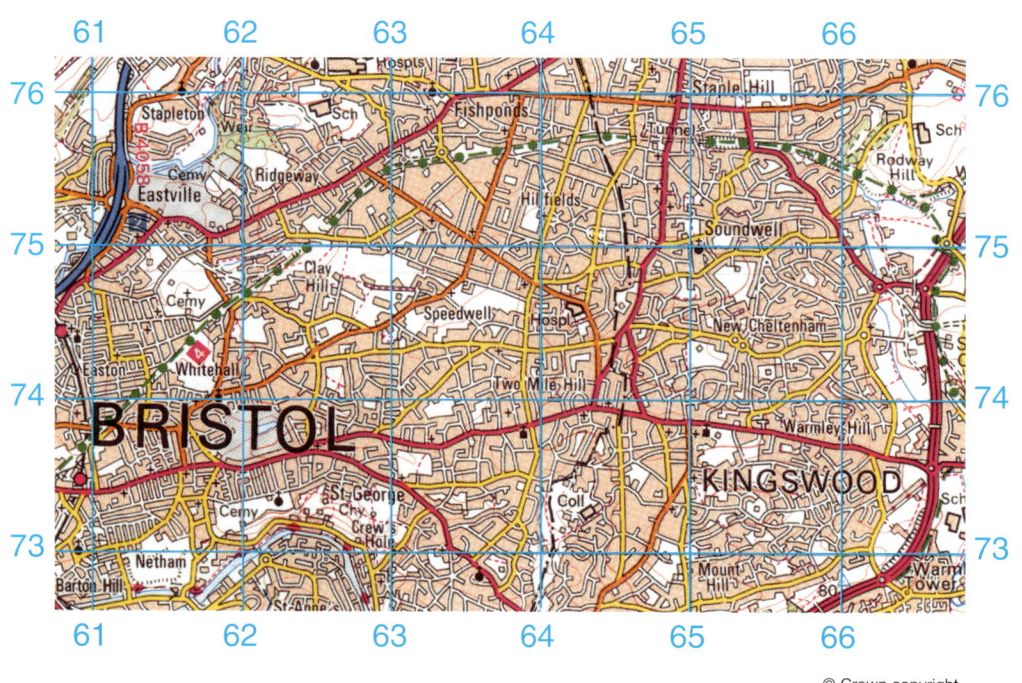

▽ **Figure 1.7** An OS 1:50 000 scale map of part of east Bristol. There is a school at 634745. It is not marked because the map is too crowded at that point.

© Crown copyright

▽ **Figure 1.8** A school is often shown on an OS map by writing Sch, but this is not always done

8 INVESTIGATING GEOGRAPHY A

Is it good to live there?

Places are always changing. Some changes can make it more attractive to live there. Other changes make people angry. The word **environment** is used to describe the features of an area and how people feel about a place. It can be hard to make the environment suitable for everyone.

△ **Figure 1.9** A vertical air photo of part of east Bristol. The school at 634745 on the OS map is in the top centre of the photo. The school is shown on the left.

Location of the vertical air photo.

Activities

Foundation

2 Write a list of the main types of land use either in your local area or the area around the school shown in Figure 1.9. This list may help you to start:

- houses
- factories
- roads
- recreation
- woods

Target

3 Write a list of the different types of land use either for your own local area or the area around the school shown in Figure 1.9. For each type of land use, write some notes to say what you think it looks like, when you think it was built and how much space it takes up in the area.

4 How might the area change in the near future? Give reasons for your answer.

Extension

5 Are there any ways in which the physical geography affects the human geography either in your local area or in the area shown in Figure 1.9?

6 Write down some questions you might want to ask about living in the area. Choose one of your own questions. What information do you think you would need to find out the answer?

1 Connecting Places 9

How can I describe a place?

Writing about a place

Writing about a place is one way to record its geography. You should:
- use accurate information
- organise it into paragraphs
- check spelling, punctuation and grammar
- use special geographical words
- include statistics (figures)
- include information you have researched
- list where you found the information
- include reasons to explain what you have described.

▷ **Figure 1.10** An oblique air view of part of the central part of London

Using statistics

Read, measure or estimate these statistics from text, photos and maps to add detail to your descriptions

length	depth
width	area
height	slope angle

Using statistics in your description

You can include statistics in your description in several ways:
- in the writing itself
- in a table
- as a graph
- on a map.

Activities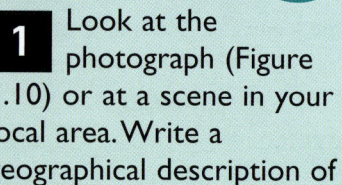

1 Look at the photograph (Figure 1.10) or at a scene in your local area. Write a geographical description of the place.

2 What evidence is there from Figure 1.10 that this is a scene from the central part of a big city?

10 INVESTIGATING GEOGRAPHY A

Sketching a scene

Drawing a **field sketch** of a place is another way to record its geography. To draw a field sketch, follow these steps:
- Begin with a frame to outline the scene you want to draw.
- Draw the main lines such as the skyline and main slopes.
- Sketch the details you want to include, using simple lines and shading.
- Print labels on or around the sketch.

▽ **Figure 1.12** The coastline at Lulworth Cove in Dorset

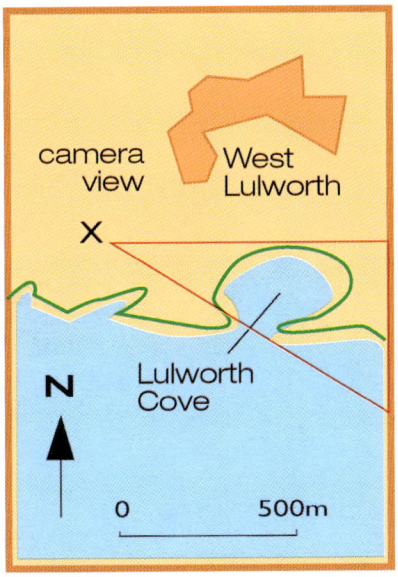

△ **Figure 1.11** Map of the scene shown in the photo. The photo was taken at point X looking east between the red lines

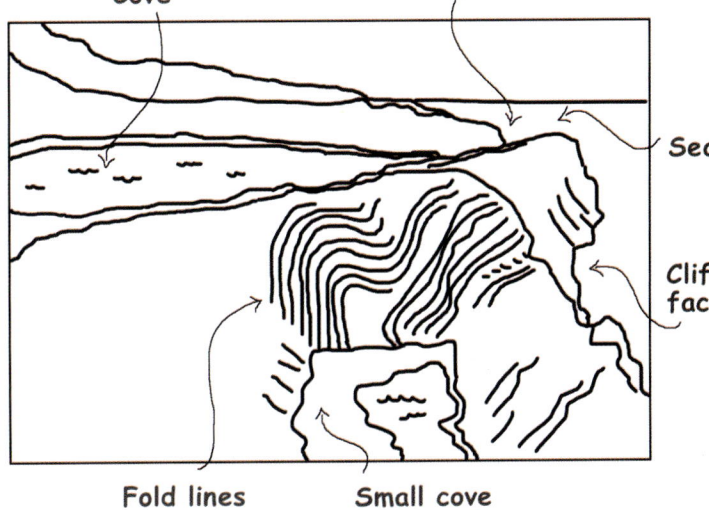

▷ **Figure 1.13** A line drawing of the coastline at Lulworth Cove, Dorset. The sketch can be completed with shading or colours

ICT activity

Make a **line drawing** of a digital photo. To do this, insert the photo into a word processor. Use the drawing tools to draw the lines then delete the photo. Add labels using Text boxes or Callouts. Then use the Select Objects tool and Group from the Draw menu to group the lines into one image.

Activities

3 Practise drawing line drawings using photos in books or magazines. Better still, practise by drawing a field sketch.

1 Connecting Places   11

How can I find other places?

What is latitude and longitude?

You have already learnt about the Global Positioning System (pages 4–5). This can give a figure for latitude and longitude for every place on the Earth. The latitude and longitude of places are usually listed in the index of an atlas.

Finding a place from its latitude and longitude is like using a grid, but it is not quite that simple. This is because the Earth is a **globe** so you cannot draw a simple grid of squares on it. The latitude lines curve around the Earth from east to west. The longitude lines curve around from north to south. This is difficult to draw on a flat map! The way a map is drawn is called the **map projection**.

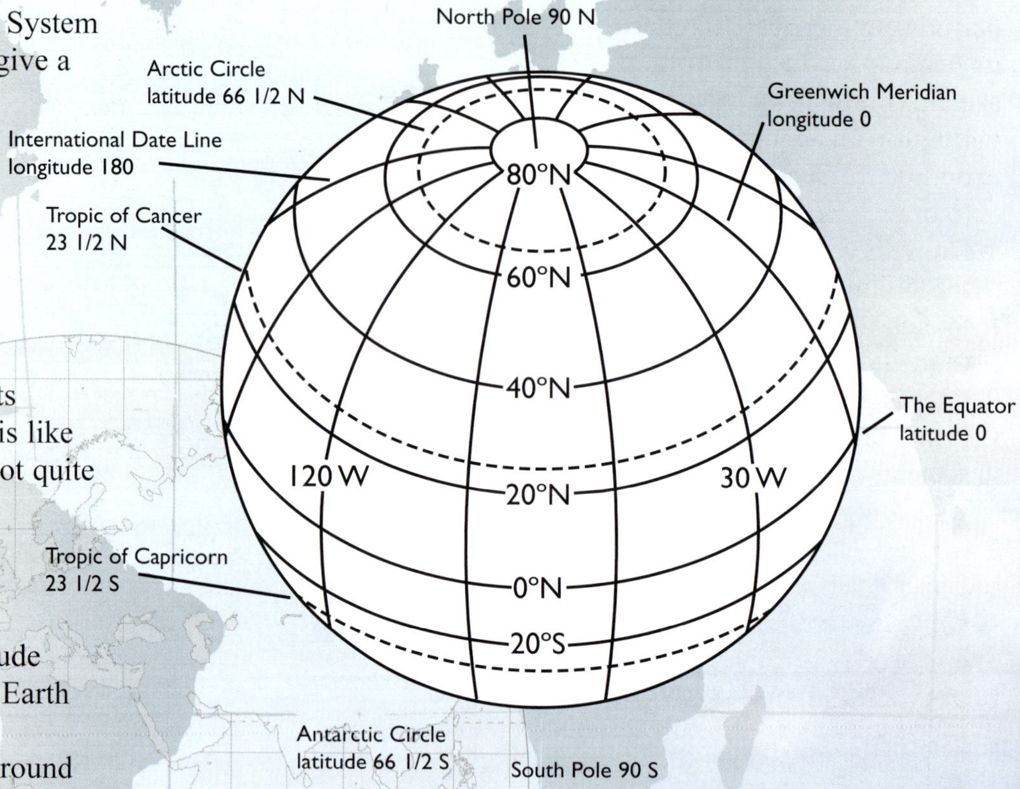

△ **Figure 1.14** The main lines of latitude and longitude

▽ **Figure 1.15** An equal area projection map of the world with lines of latitude and longitude

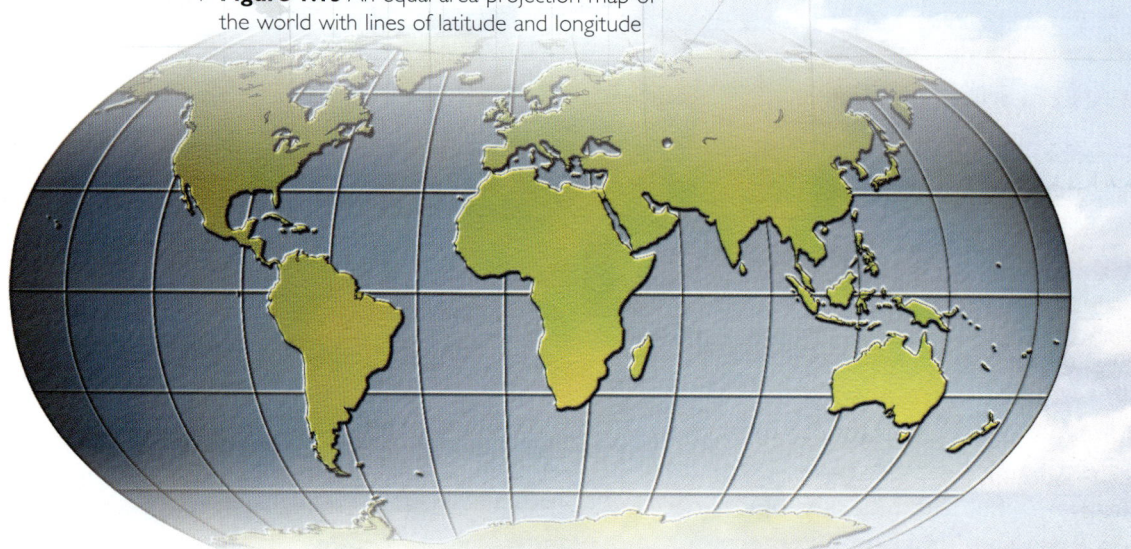

12 INVESTIGATING GEOGRAPHY A

How does latitude and longitude help find a place?

The **Equator** is a line of latitude drawn around the widest part of the globe. It is at latitude 0. Any place not on the Equator must be either north or south of it.

The **Greenwich Meridian** is a line of longitude drawn from the North Pole to the South Pole. It is at longitude 0. All places that are not on this line must be either east or west of it.

So latitude and longitude references tell you if a place is north or south of latitude 0 and east or west of longitude 0. The figures are measured in degrees.

You may also know that each degree is subdivided into minutes, then into smaller units called seconds.

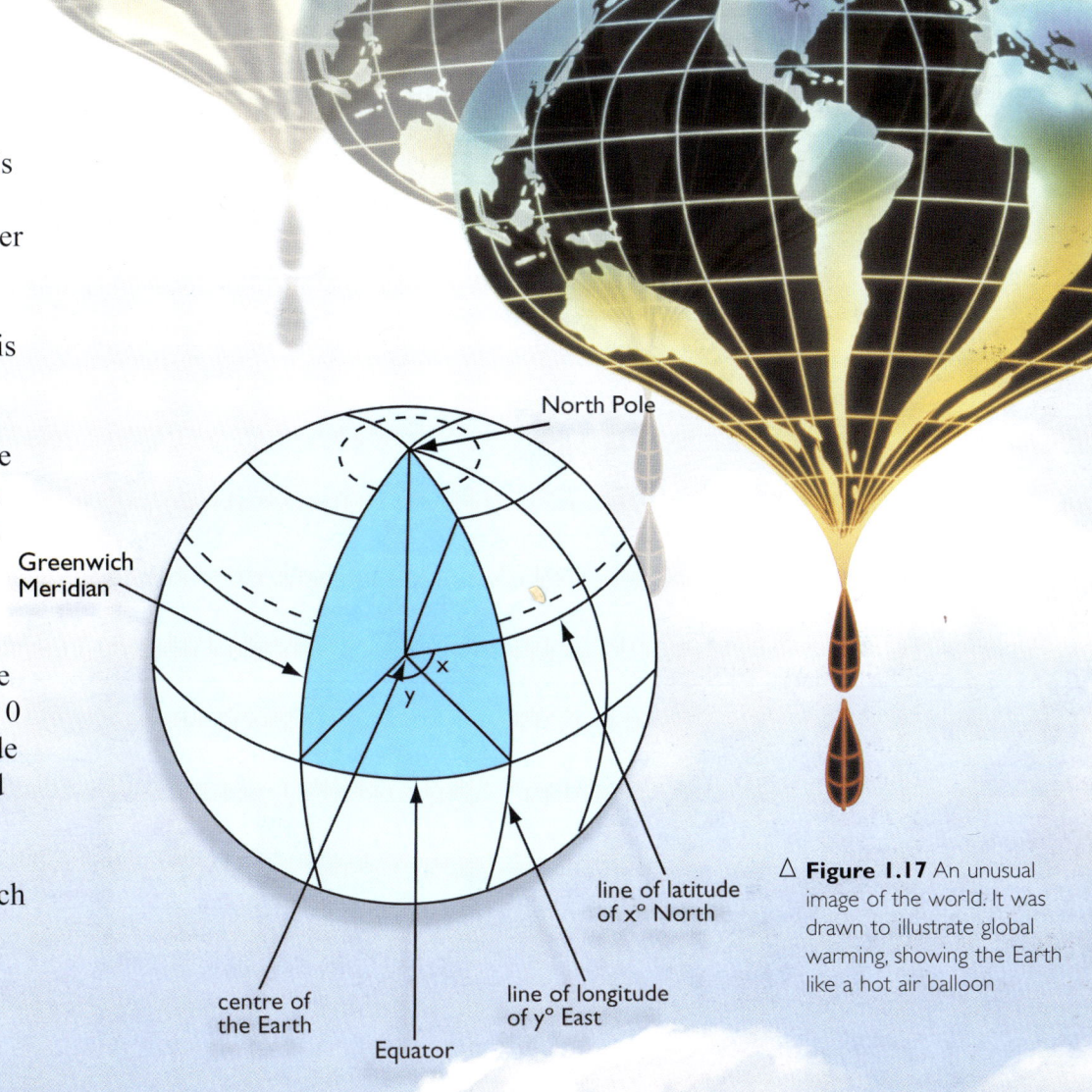

△ **Figure 1.16** How to draw latitude and longitude lines

△ **Figure 1.17** An unusual image of the world. It was drawn to illustrate global warming, showing the Earth like a hot air balloon

Activities

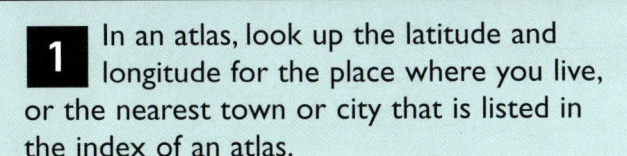

1 In an atlas, look up the latitude and longitude for the place where you live, or the nearest town or city that is listed in the index of an atlas.

2 For each of these places, write down their figures for latitude and longitude:
- New York
- Calcutta
- Cairo

You can estimate their positions in degrees between the major lines that have been drawn. For example if only latitudes 30N and 35N have been drawn, you can estimate where latitude 33N would be.

3 Describe how lines of latitude and longitude have been drawn in some atlas maps. See if they curve.

1 Connecting Places

Where am I linked to?

Global links

Every time you use the Internet, you are part of a system that links anyone anywhere on the Earth who has a computer, a modem and a telephone line. Distance between places is not a problem if you want to contact people in other places. Even the cost is no more than a local telephone call.

Figure 1.20 A cybercafe in Cambodia where you can send emails, search the World Wide Web, and have a drink

Figure 1.18 People who are connected to the Internet

Figure 1.19 The calls I make to people

Country	Internet users (millions)	Population in millions
U.S.	134.6	288
Japan	33.9	127
China	22.5	1307
Germany	19.9	82
South Korea	19.0	47
U.K.	16.8	59
Canada	15.4	31
Italy	12.5	58
France	9.0	59
Australia	7.6	20
Russia	7.5	143
Taiwan	7.0	23
Spain	5.6	41
Netherlands	5.5	16
Sweden	4.4	9

Figure 1.21 The top 15 countries for Internet use.

Links with other places

You only have to look around you to see ways your place is connected to other places. In your own home, there are foods and other things that come from different places. Some come from other parts of your country. Others come from different countries. As you go to school, you will see cars that were made in many different countries. Even your school can not be run without links to other places. Books and other resources, water, electricity and food have to come from other places.

Activities

1 Look at the map (Figure 1.18) showing where people are linked to the Internet. Describe and give some reasons for the pattern that you can see.

14 INVESTIGATING GEOGRAPHY A

Is it good to have links?

There would be less variety, less choice and it would not be as interesting if you only used things and met people from the local area. But remember also that it takes energy to move people and goods on trains, lorries and planes. This can cause air pollution. At Luton airport near London, passengers have been asked to pay extra for their flight because of the damage that the aircraft will do to the environment. It may also happen that if someone in one country makes the goods, then someone in another country might lose their job.

▽ **Figure 1.22** A holiday in Barbados

▽ **Figure 1.23** People who live near airports suffer from aircraft noise as other people go on holiday

ICT activity

At Luton airport, passengers are being asked to pay extra for their flight because using aircraft fuel puts carbon dioxide into the air. The money will be used to plant trees in the Luton area. Trees can soak up carbon dioxide.

Use the Luton airport web site to find out more about the airport's plans to take care of the environment:
www.london-luton.com

Activities

Foundation

2 Write down something that you own or use that was made in a different country. Which country did it come from? How does the item help you in your daily life? Do you think this item could have been made in the area where you live? Explain your answer.

Target

3 Describe some ways that your own life would be different if you did not have links with other places. Do you think that your life both now and in the future will be made better or worse by having links with other countries?

Extension

4 Use items from the news to give examples of how links with other places can bring both benefits and sometimes problems. Your answers can refer both to your own life and to other people's. You could include your own view about the idea used at Luton airport to pay more for a flight.

1 Connecting Places 15

What questions can I ask?

What's the same and what's different?

One question you can ask is how places are similar and how they are different. It can help you to understand places if you can **compare** them to see how they are similar, and **contrast** them to see how they are different.

You can organise your ideas by using a list of headings. There are also some special geographical words that you can use. Sometimes, however, a word used in geography can mean something different in another subject. You can also use adjectives to describe places. In geography, it is always better to try to use a statistic. What is big in one place may be small somewhere else.

Headings to compare places	Examples of words
Relief (shape of the land)	plains, valley, hill
Drainage (rivers)	stream, river, tributary
Climate and weather	hurricane, clouds, pressure
Vegetation	forest, grassland, crops
Population	densely populated, multi-racial, migration
Work	industry, farming, services
Recreation and leisure	park, leisure centre, stadium
Transport	airport, motorway, navigation

▽ Figure 1.24 Goosekill Bridge, Castleton, Derbyshire

Adjectives to describe places

big	low
wide	narrow
rough	gentle
large	small
steep	high
smooth	deep

▽ Figure 1.25 The river Thames in London

Activities

1. Compare and contrast the two photographs, Figure 1.24 and 1.25. Try to include some statistics, even if you have to estimate them.

2. Look up some statistics to compare some features in the UK with the same feature elsewhere in the world, e.g:
   - the highest mountain
   - the longest river
   - the biggest city.

What questions will I ask?

A **geographical enquiry** is when you ask a question, research information, present your information then answer the question. **Primary sources of evidence** are information you collect by visiting a place and carrying out **fieldwork**. If you cannot do that, you might be able to find the information from **secondary sources** such as in reference books and the World Wide Web.

❯ The steps for enquiry

- Ask a question.
- List the information you think you need to answer it.
- Research the information.
- Select, record and present the information.
- Answer the question.

Activities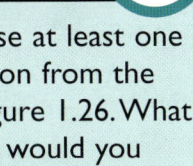

3 Choose at least one question from the photo in Figure 1.26. What information would you need to answer it and how would you get it?

▲ **Figure 1.26** A scene in the UK Lake District National Park

Questions in geography	Information needed
Where is a place?	Describe its position and say if it relates to other places in a pattern.
What is there and what does a place look like?	A list and description of the features at a place. This can be done to compare and contrast places.
How did the place get to look as it does?	A set of reasons that explain why the place looks as it does. This can include reasons from both the past and the present.
Why might people want to live there?	A list of features in the place with an understanding of how people feel about those features.
Should a place be changed?	Your views about whether the changes would be a benefit or would cause problems.

◁ **Figure 1.27** A student doing fieldwork

1 Connecting Places

Is information always right?

Is it the truth?

Not everything you read about a place is true. Information can sometimes be wrong if someone makes a mistake. Sometimes the information is only partly true. This can be when the person who wrote it is trying to persuade you of something. This information is likely to be **biased**. It may include some things but leave out something else. Even a photo may not show the whole truth. The photos and text about the holiday resort of Portinatx in Ibiza show how careful you need to be when you choose information about a place.

Activities

1. Look at the information and photos about Portinatx in Ibiza. What are the good and bad things they tell you about the resort?

◁ Figure 1.28 The beach at Portinatx

▷ New holiday villas being built

▽ A tourist shop and holiday flats

18 see ibiza

Portinatx

The bay offers magnificent panoramic views, crystalline clear water, high rocky shorelines and a seabed of fine, white sand. The amazing panoramic views of this picturesque bay are a wonderful combination of diamond bright, translucent sea reflected in myriad shades of blue. There is a games centre with bowling and pool tables. There are music bars, pubs, quiz evenings and a surprisingly active nightlife scene.

– Information from a website advertising a holiday in Spain.

◁ A street in Portinatx

18 INVESTIGATING GEOGRAPHY A

How can I check the information?

To check on whether the information is either true or fair, you need to know about where it came from. The World Wide Web can be a special problem. Anyone can set up a website and put anything on it. These are reasons why you should always include a list of where your information came from. This is what a **bibliography** is for.

▷ **Figure 1.30** The logo of the Alaska Wilderness League. This is an organisation that wants to conserve the environment in the area as it is: www.alaskawild.org/

△ **Figure 1.29** The environment in the Arctic National Wildlife Refuge in Alaska

❯ What to check

- When it was written: is the information out of date?
- Where the information came from: has the writer ever been there?
- Who wrote it: can you trust the writer to be accurate and fair?
- Why was it written: does the writer want to persuade you?

2   see **alaska**

The Arctic National Wildlife Refuge

British Petroleum and other multi-national oil companies insist on drilling in the Arctic National Wildlife Refuge, on the last five percent of Alaska's northern coastal land not already open to oil exploration or drilling. Its 19 million acres comprise one of the last places on earth where an intact expanse of arctic and subarctic lands remain protected. It is considered the crown jewel of America's national Wildlife Refuge System. And yet this truly undisturbed wilderness is today in grave danger of being destroyed by those seeking whatever oil might lie beneath its fragile tundra.

△ **Figure 1.31** This text was written by the Alaskan Wilderness League

Activities

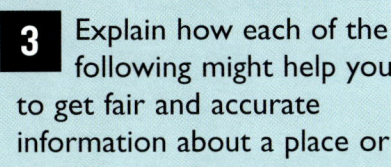

2 Read what the Alaska Wilderness League say about drilling for oil in Alaska (Figure 1.31). Do you think that what they say is the truth? Use the resources on this page to explain your answer. You could also find out more about drilling for oil in Alaska on the Alaska Wilderness League's website and other websites.

3 Explain how each of the following might help you to get fair and accurate information about a place or issue:
- information from different sources
- different types of information
- the amount of information.

1 Connecting Places   19

Assessment tasks

Background

You work for a company called Image Makers. The company helps to plan and advertise leisure and recreation facilities. The district council in your area wants to improve the leisure and recreation facilities for people who live in the area. They have given your company the job of doing this.

Image Makers offers a *Standard* (Target task) and a *Premier* (Extension task) level of service to its clients. The *Premier* service offers more, but it costs more to buy.

Before you begin this task, you should decide on:
- which level of service the council is buying from you
- if you can work as a team with the work divided between you.

(Your teacher will help you to make these decisions).

△ **Figure 1.32** The Image Makers' Company

How to write your report

The report should be set out in four parts. You should add your own ideas in every part. See page 21–2 for further details.

A: The planning background
This part gives background information about the area to help plan the kind of leisure and recreation facilities that people will want to use.

B: Existing facilities and access
This part aims to describe the facilities there now and how to get to them.

C: Publicity
In this part, you will provide ideas about how to advertise the facilities.

D: New ideas
This section is where you can present some ideas for new facilities or how to change what is already there.

Target task

Write a *Standard Service* report for the council. Guidance on page 21 shows you what to include.

Extension task

Write a *Premium Service* report for the council. Guidance on page 22 shows you what to include.

20 INVESTIGATING GEOGRAPHY A

Writing the report

Target tasks – Standard Service

A: The planning background
- Give information about the total population, land use and how the area has changed.
- Give some views about what people might want.
- The information can be presented as short descriptions, tables of figures or basic graphs.

B: Existing facilities and access
- Give a list of the different types of leisure and recreation facilities. Divide them into indoor and outdoor facilities.
- Give brief details of what can be done at each facility listed.
- Give information about how people might get to some of the facilities. This could include bus routes, footpaths and car parks.
- Mark the facilities on a map. You could use four-figure grid references to locate the facilities.
- Write some notes to describe the pattern of facilities in the area.

C: Publicity
- Make a leaflet or short brochure to advertise the facilities.
- Think of a slogan that would draw attention to the facilities.
- Include some sketches or photos of some of the facilities.

D: New Ideas
- Give at least one idea for a new leisure and recreation facility for the area. You could think about whether the area's physical geography can be used, for example if there is a river. There could be a new swimming pool or a historic trail.
- Give reasons why it might be successful.

◁ **Figure 1.33**
A local park
An indoor sports centre
A play area for young children
A restored canal and footpath
Tennis courts
A fun fair
A leisure complex

1 Connecting Places

Writing the report

Extension task - Premier Service

A: The planning background
- Give information about the area's population, including their age and other details.
- Give information about the general features of the area including its physical features and land use.
- Draw up a questionnaire that could be used to ask people about what they want. This should have no more than 10 questions.
- Include some information about the human and physical geography of the surrounding counties. This may help to plan facilities that might attract people to come into your area. You can use an atlas to do this.
- The information can be presented as descriptions that include statistics and other details. A good range of graphs and maps should be drawn.

B: Existing facilities and access
- Give a list of the different types of leisure and recreation facilities. Put them into groups such as indoors or outdoors and the cost of using them.
- Write comments about the quality of the facilities. Also mention the people who use them, such as their age and how often they are used.
- Mark the facilities on maps using keys to show how they are different. You could use six-figure grid references to pinpoint the facilities.
- Give information about how people might get to some of the facilities. This could include bus routes and how often the service runs, roads, car parks and cycle lanes. You should do this for some of the facilities but not for all of them.
- You should include main roads and railway stations to show how visitors from outside the local area can get there.
- Write some comments to describe and explain the pattern of the facilities across the area.

C: Publicity
- Make some publicity material to advertise the facilities. You could create a brochure, a script for a radio broadcast or a story board for a television advert.
- Try to make an image for the area. Perhaps someone famous lived in the area or a book or television programme was based there. Use this to make the place sound more attractive.

D: New Ideas
- Give at least one idea for new and improved facilities.
- Mark it on a map.
- Explain why it might be successful. Write some comments about the effects it might have on people who live in the area near it.

22 INVESTIGATING GEOGRAPHY A

Review

What have I learnt in this section?

In this section, you have learnt about three main things:
- How to study places to see what is there and to think about some ways in which places are linked.
- How to use maps and photographs to find out about where places are and what is there.
- How to ask geographical questions and develop some of the skills required to research the information you need to answer those questions.

Activities

1 Which is the odd one out from these lists? Use an atlas to find out. Explain your answers.

List A
England
London
Wales
Scotland

List C
Severn
Trent
Danube
Thames

List B
Bristol
Sheffield
Wales
Norwich

2 Find the latitude and longitude of each of these places. Then locate them in an atlas.
- Athens
- Berlin
- Madrid
- Paris
- Vienna

3 Study the photograph, Figure 1.34.
a Make a line drawing of it. Add labels to point to the physical and human features that you can identify.
b Write down at least three questions that you might want to ask about the scene. The questions can be about the physical geography, the human geography or a question about the environment.

△ **Figure 1.34** A scene in South West England

4 Does the place where you live or a place near to it have a twin town? If it does, use your research skills to find out some ways that it is similar and some ways that it is different to where you live. If not, you can choose a place yourself or your teacher can choose for you. Find out about:
- the people who live there
- what its position is, if it is near the sea, inland, in mountains or plains
- the name of the biggest river that flows through it
- what people do for a living
- what people might do for recreation

You can find some of the answers in an atlas. For more information, use reference books, CD-Roms and the World Wide Web.

5 For the place you have studied in Activity 4, describe some ways that you think it might be linked to other places, both in the same country and in other countries. Are there any advantages and problems these links might bring?

1 Connecting Places

2 Development: Change in Contrasting Localities

Change for the better?

What do you think?

△ **Figure 2.1** A concept map of trade

Activities

1 Take a moment to think about what you already know about these themes and nations:
   development   Ghana   Germany   England

For each one produce your own concept map to show your knowledge and opinions to others. Do this task completely on your own. On this page is a concept map to show what someone felt they knew about the theme of trade. It might give you some ideas how to set yours out.

2 Compare your concept map with the concept maps of two other people in your class. Make a list of the words or phrases that you had that were the same, and a list of the things that were different. You can then compare your group's list with those of the whole class. You could record these results in a spreadsheet and/or graph. What was surprising, interesting, or unusual about the whole class results?
Keep this information handy – you will need to use it later!

24 INVESTIGATING GEOGRAPHY A

△ Figure 2.2

△ Figure 2.3

▽ Figure 2.4

△ Figure 2.5

△ Figure 2.6

△ Figure 2.7

Activities

3 Spend a few minutes looking at the photos on this page.

4 Two of the photos belong to a place in Germany, two to a place in Ghana, and two to a place in England. Try to decide which two photos go together for each place, note down what you think, and explain why you made your choices. For example, Figure 2.2 belongs to …… because ……

5 How do your choices compare to reality? Why do you think that your choices were right or wrong?

2 Development: Change in Contrasting Localities   25

So what about these places?

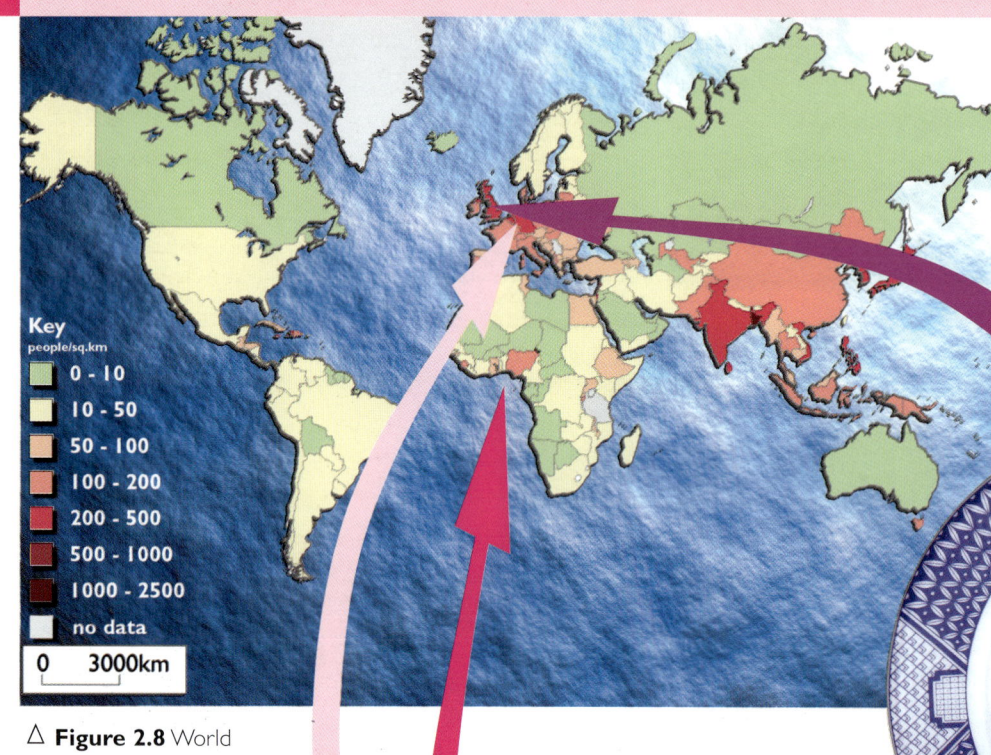

△ **Figure 2.8** World population density, 1996

▽ **Figure 2.12** Plate produced by the Stoke-on-Trent potteries, now in the Gladstone Museum, Longton

△ **Figure 2.9** Nordbad swimming pool, restored as part of a development project in the Ausere region of Dresden

▷ **Figure 2.10** Gold produced from Ghanaian gold mines, including Obuasi, in the Ashanti region

Development – A shorthand definition

Development is about people

Development is about people making choices based on values

Development is about people making choices based on values about the quality of life.

△ Figure 2.11

26 INVESTIGATING GEOGRAPHY A

Investigating choices

In this chapter you will explore the theme of development mainly at the local scale. Local means an area about the size of the catchment area of your school. It is a small area, but still really complex. Lots happens there.

Development is one of the themes that we study in geography. It is a difficult idea to define. Figure 2.11 talks about values and quality of life. Values can refer to a person's set of beliefs and ideas. These can be to do with how to make money, how to treat people, or how to treat the environment. Quality of life is about how well people live. It is not always easy to measure this. It can be as much about how good people feel their life is as about things like access to water and health care.

We are going to investigate some of these ideas in three places. Each place is somebody else's local area. The three places are shown on the map opposite (Figure 2.8).

Choices and places

Making choices in a careful way is important. Choices often change people and places. In Obuasi, Ausere and Stoke, we are going to find out about some significant planned changes to these places. We are going to think about how changes affect individuals, so we are going to start by considering you as an individual and some of the choices that you might make.

Activities

1 a Look at the map and images opposite. You have the choice to buy either: the gold from Ghana; the plate from Stoke; or a holiday in Dresden. They all cost roughly the same. Use the boxes below to help you explain your choices.

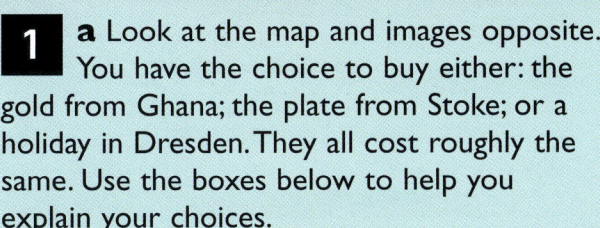

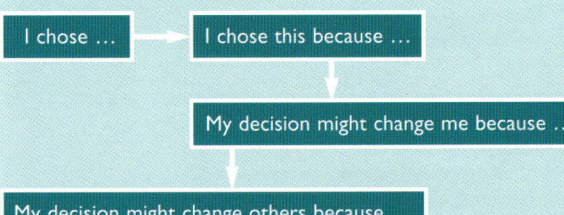

b Now try to decide which of these boxes gives you some information about:
- people
- choices
- values
- quality of life

Either label your boxes, or write to explain your answers. You can use more than one label for each box.

2 a Look carefully at the population map in Figure 2.8. Use this and an atlas to help you to complete the table below.

Local area	Country	People/sq km	Continent
Obuasi			
Stoke			
Ausere			

b Use your completed table to help you to correct the following paragraph. (Page 28 explains what is meant by population density.)

Ghana is on the continent of America/Africa. It is a much smaller/larger continent than Europe. England and Germany both have the same/different population densities. This is higher/lower than Ghana.

2 Development: Change in Contrasting Localities

What does quality of life mean?

Population density can tell us about how crowded a place is. It does not tell us about how well the people live in that place. One of the ways that we can think about development is to investigate people's quality of life. On the day that you were born, so were around another 365 000 people. Some may have very similar lives to you, others very different. These similarities and differences will be caused by a number of reasons; some to do with money; some to do with our families and communities; some to do with the environments where we live. All these are factors that we think about when we investigate development. In all countries there are people with needs. There is not enough money or skill available in the world at present to undertake all the development which people need. Choices have to be made.

Development projects

On the next few pages we explore three development projects and investigate how people's quality of life has been changed by each of the projects. Before we look at these local-scale examples in more detail, let's explore the idea of 'quality of life' a little further. In Ghana 42%, in Germany 16%, and in England 19% of the population are under 15. Their concerns about their future and quality of life are important in terms of development and change.

Young people's concerns for the future

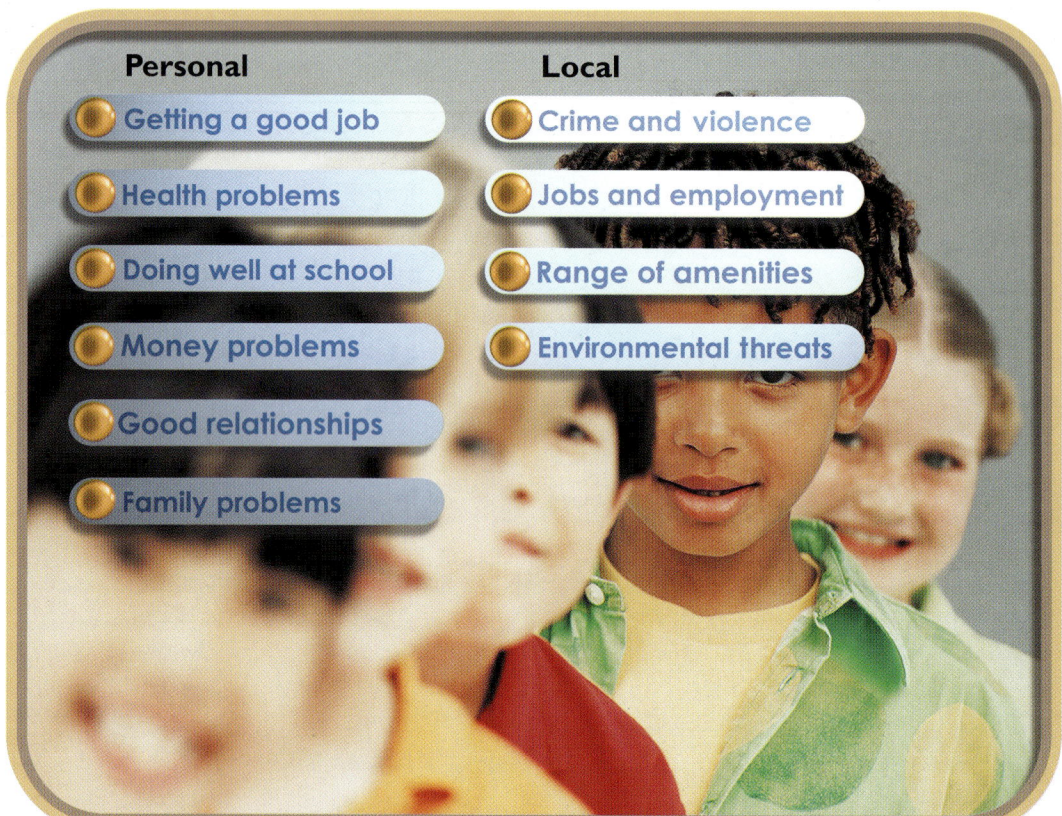

Personal
- Getting a good job
- Health problems
- Doing well at school
- Money problems
- Good relationships
- Family problems

Local
- Crime and violence
- Jobs and employment
- Range of amenities
- Environmental threats

Source; Hicks, D & Holden, C (eds), **Visions of the Future, Why We Need to Teach for Tomorrow**, Stoke on Trent, Trentham.

28 INVESTIGATING GEOGRAPHY A

▷ **Figure 2.13** Quality of Life frame

Activities

1 Thinking about yourself – do you agree with the young people's concerns for the future? Are there any that you would add?

2 a In a group of three, copy out all of the young people's concerns for the future statements, except for 'jobs and employment', onto nine small pieces of paper or card. Thinking about your quality of life in your area, talk about what each statement means to you. Now try to arrange the statements in a diamond pattern, ordering them carefully so that all of you are happy with the decisions. The card chosen as the most important is ranked at the top of the diamond, the least important at the base, and the others between. Each person in your group needs to make a copy of your final pattern.

b On your own use a large copy of the quality of life frame (Figure 2.13) to note down your decisions and the reasons for your decisions.

c By doing these activities you have explored some of the difficulties of trying to define development and quality of life. Your own personal values

will have influenced your choices. Take a few moments to think about the skills that you have used carrying out these activities. It is worth remembering them, because you will be doing similar work again, and you will want to do it better!

2 Development: Change in Contrasting Localities 29

So what about values and geography?

In the shorthand definition of development on page 26, values were mentioned. All of us have our own set of views. Some of these come from outside influences – such as whom we mix with, where we live, the ideas that we get from television – and some of our views are to do with our own character. All of us have a different awareness of other places. People's views about and the values they attach to places is another difficult area for geographers to investigate. You are going to do this by thinking about your own place, and some of your reactions to data about development.

Scale

Most of the information in this chapter is about local areas and is given at the local scale. Sometimes it is important to think about how these local areas are linked to other places. In each of these places live individual people, like you. Each of these areas is part of a region, and part of a nation. For example, individuals live in Obuasi, in the Ashanti region of Ghana. In this section you as an individual (personal scale) are going to respond to some national data (national scale) about communications. Communication is a way that we gain knowledge and develop our values. Communication is part of our personal development.

▽ **Figure 2.14** Table to show communications data

Country	1990 Main telephone lines per 1 000 people	1998 Main telephone lines per 1 000 people	1990 Mobile phone subscribers per 1 000 people	1998 Mobile phone subscribers per 1 000 people	1990 Television per 1 000 people	1998 Television per 1 000 people	1990 Personal Computers per 1 000 people	1998 Personal Computers per 1 000 people
United Kingdom	441	556	19	252	433	645	108	263
Germany	441	567	4	170	525	580	91	305
Ghana	3	8	0	1	15	115	0	2

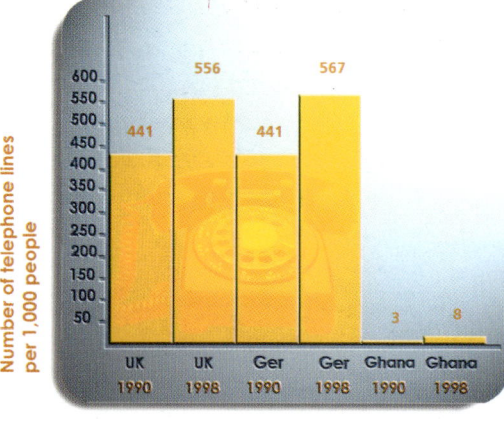

◁ **Figure 2.15** A bar chart to show main telephone lines per 1 000 people

▷ **Figure 2.16** A line graph to show number of televisions per 1 000 people

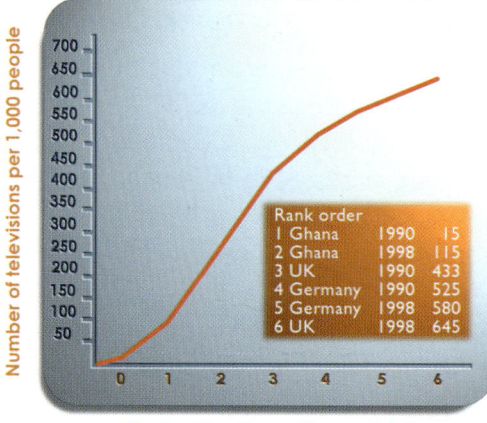

30 INVESTIGATING GEOGRAPHY A

Activities

Foundation

1 Look at the data in Table 2.14 on page 30 and the two graphs 2.15 and 2.16. Look carefully at the scales to work out how they have been drawn.

2 On graph paper, draw a bar chart similar to 2.15 to show the number of mobile phone subscribers in Germany, Ghana and the United Kingdom in 1990 and 1998.

3 On graph paper draw a line graph similar to 2.16 to show the number of personal computers per 1 000 people. Why do you think the figure for Ghana in 1990 might be an average rather than an absolute zero?

4 What do you think all four graphs, the two on this page and the two that you have drawn, tell you about communication?

Target

5 Draw a line graph similar to Figure 2.16 to show the number of personal computers per 1 000 people. See if you can use it to complete the following paragraph:

In the years between 1990 and 1998, twice as many people had access to a computer in ... Roughly three times as many people had access to a computer in ... Two and a half as many people had access to a computer in ...

6 Consider your line graph, Figures 2.15, 2.16 and the data from Figure 2.14. What do you think that the data is saying about access to information? You may wish to use the prompts:

I think that ... I also think ... Another thing that I think is ...

7 Share what you think with two other people in your class. Do you want to go back and add or change anything that you have written?

Extension

8 Draw a line graph similar to Figure 2.16 to show the number of personal computers per 1 000 people. Where would you place the following statements on your line graph:

a More people shop on the Internet than ever before.
b More people in rich countries can use the Internet.
c It is now easier to get access to a computer; eight years ago it was almost impossible.

9 When you have chosen where your statements will go, swap with someone else to see where theirs went. There are several places on your line graph where these statements could be true. It shows you that statistics need to be handled with care, and that there can sometimes be different ways to use them.

2 Development: Change in Contrasting Localities 31

Activities

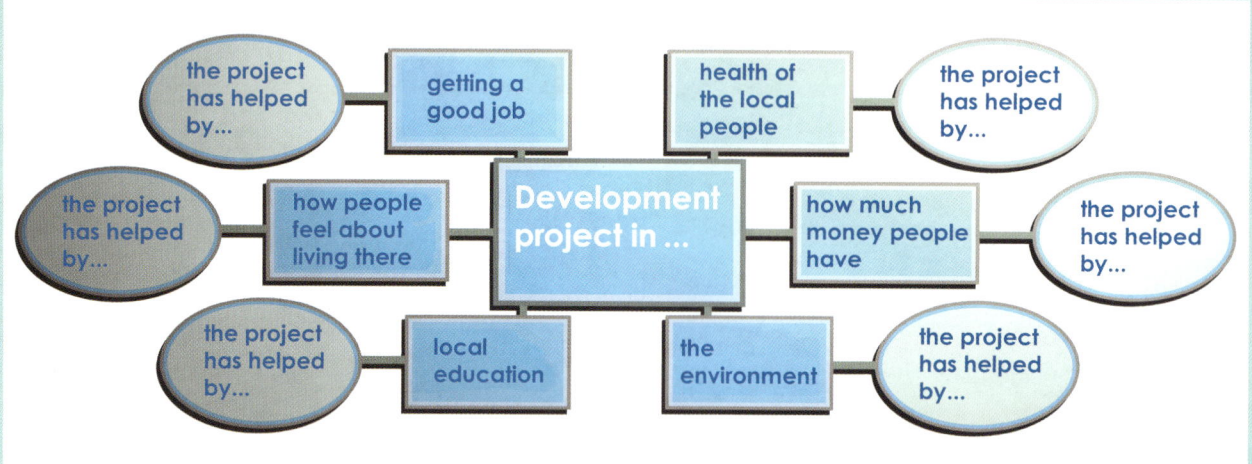

△ **Figure 2.17** Development Factfile

You will need to use the information on pages 34 and 35 for Stoke, 36 and 37 for Obuasi and 38 and 39 for Ausere, as well as any other information that you can find in this chapter or any other resources.

1 You will need to work in a group of three. Your task is to investigate one of the case studies. You will be told which one. For your case study you need to gather the following information to complete a development factfile like the one shown above.

All members of your group need to have a note in some form of this information.

2 You now need to form new groups of three, so that one of you has the investigation from Stoke, another the investigation from Obuasi, and the third, the one from Ausere. Now you need to think about sharing the information that you have gathered. To do this you need to complete columns 1–3 on the information grid below.

How has the development helped to change.........	1. Obuasi	2. Stoke on Trent	3. Ausere	4. What I think is similar	5. What I think is different
the chances of getting a good job					
the health of the people who live there					
how much money people have					
the environment					
how people feel about living there					

32 INVESTIGATING GEOGRAPHY A

Activities

Foundation

3 Working on your own, try to complete columns 4 and 5 of your grid. You need to think about how the reasons for the changes, or the results of the changes, in these three places may be similar and how they may be different from each other.

4 Chose one of the three places that you have investigated. For that place decide whether or not you think that the development project was a change for the better. Use the Reasons and Conclusions frame below to help you to draft your answer.

Reasons and Conclusions

Conclusions

Reasons

◁ **Figure 2.18** Reasons and Conclusions frame

Target

5 Complete the Reasons and Conclusions frame in Figure 2.18 using the information on Obuasi and one other project of your choice, decide whether or not the developments have brought about changes for the better in the two areas.

6 Complete columns 4 and 5 of your grid. If the European Union wanted your advice about the projects in Dresden and Stoke, how would you answer these questions:

Have we done the right thing?
Have we done enough?
Has life got better for people in those places?

Extension

7 Complete columns 4 and 5 of your grid.

8 Use the ideas from your grid to copy and complete the **Venn diagram**.

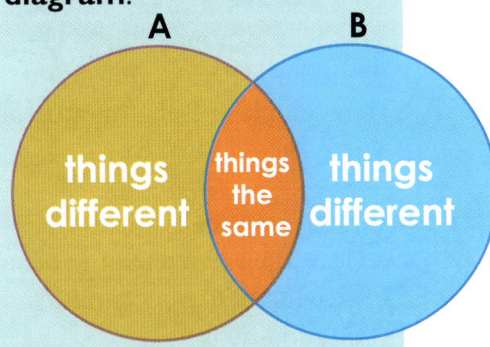

△ **Figure 2.19** Venn diagram for things the same and things different

9 Using your completed Venn diagram, draw up a list of features that you think are needed for a successful development project.

10 Use this list and the Reasons and Conclusions frame to draft a document. This document is to help you to respond to this statement:

When money is given to an area, it makes an already poor area more dependent on outside people, keeping the area at a disadvantage.

You could write your response, or tape or video it. Alternatively you could produce a poster or use your ICT skills to produce a report.

2 Development: Change in Contrasting Localities 33

Is this development of a local area?
The Ceramics Quarter, Stoke-on-Trent

❯ Where?
The project focused on a run-down industrial area of Longton in the south of the city of Stoke-on-Trent. This is an area which is traditionally associated with ceramics.

❯ What?
This was a project funded by the European Regional Development Fund. It aimed to **redevelop** the Longton area of Stoke-on-Trent. The project aimed to:

- redevelop an historic industrial area
- develop a new ceramic design centre
- provide new opportunities for training and employment
- conserve the areas' industrial heritage
- attract investment and people to the area
- create new arts and cultural facilities
- show other European towns and cities how to **regenerate** their industrial areas.

❯ Why?
During the last 150 years, the city's **landscape** had been changed by coal mining, clay extraction, iron and steel works, pottery waste tips and widespread pollution. This had led to the following problems:
- poor image, **environmental decay**
- congestion and pollution
- poor health, low income, low expectations, and low levels of educational achievement
- an unbalanced economy, which was over dependent on **traditional industries**
- unemployment – particularly in the ceramics industry.

◁ **Figure 2.20** Neglected St James's School building, Longton, Stoke-on-Trent

❯ When?
The work started in January 1992, the first phase was finished in 1995 with another phase progressing through the early years of the 21st century.

❯ How?
The project's actions involved:

△ **Figure 2.21** The Hothouse design centre

- Renovating and converting an old school building into a 'state of the art' ceramic design centre, the 'Hothouse'. New facilities include a range of units and workshops providing accommodation for industrial design studios, a computer-aided design bureau, a kiln room, a conference suite and a management studio. The project intended to show how traditional industries such as ceramics could be redeveloped by using technology and to show how important the design aspects of the industry are. The Hothouse is in a Victorian school building that was in danger of being demolished.
- Converting a vacant industrial building (Roslyn works) to provide craft workshop space for artists and crafts people.
- Restoring and upgrading the Gladstone Pottery Museum into a major tourist attraction.
- Implementing environmental improvement schemes including face lifts to fronts of local buildings, lighting pavements and landscaping.
- Running a training programme in co-operation with Staffordshire Training and Enterprise Council to provide training and employment opportunities in building and environmental skills.

34 INVESTIGATING GEOGRAPHY A

FACT FILE: THE CERAMICS QUARTER, LONGTON

The number of jobs in the pottery industry has fallen from 55 000 in 1962 to 18 600 in 1995

The Ceramic Quarter project was successful in generating employment.

52 jobs have been created.

164 jobs have been safeguarded.

81 businesses have received help with accommodation.

Raised profile of the city of Stoke-on-Trent in Europe.

Increased visitor numbers to the Gladstone Pottery Museum from 35 000 to 50 000 per year.

ICT links

Some useful websites:

www.thisisstaffordshire.co.uk

www.inforegio.org/urban/upp/src/Bullet05.htm

www.stoke.gov.uk

▽ **Figure 2.22** Outline map of Britain

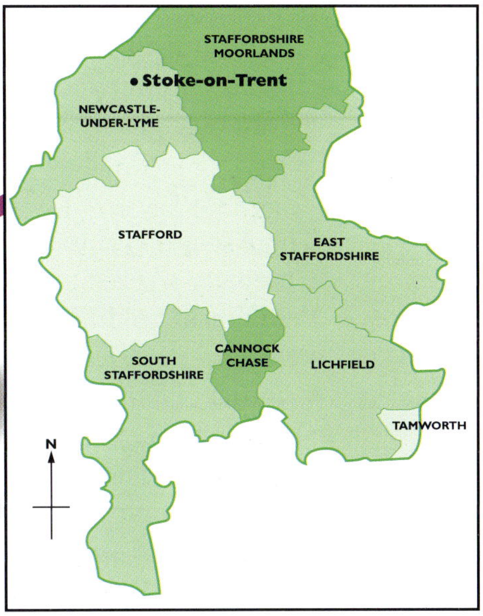

△ **Figure 2.23** Staffordshire, with Stoke-on-Trent

▽ **Figure 2.24** An OS extract showing Longton and the Ceramics Quarter Explorer 258 1: 25 000

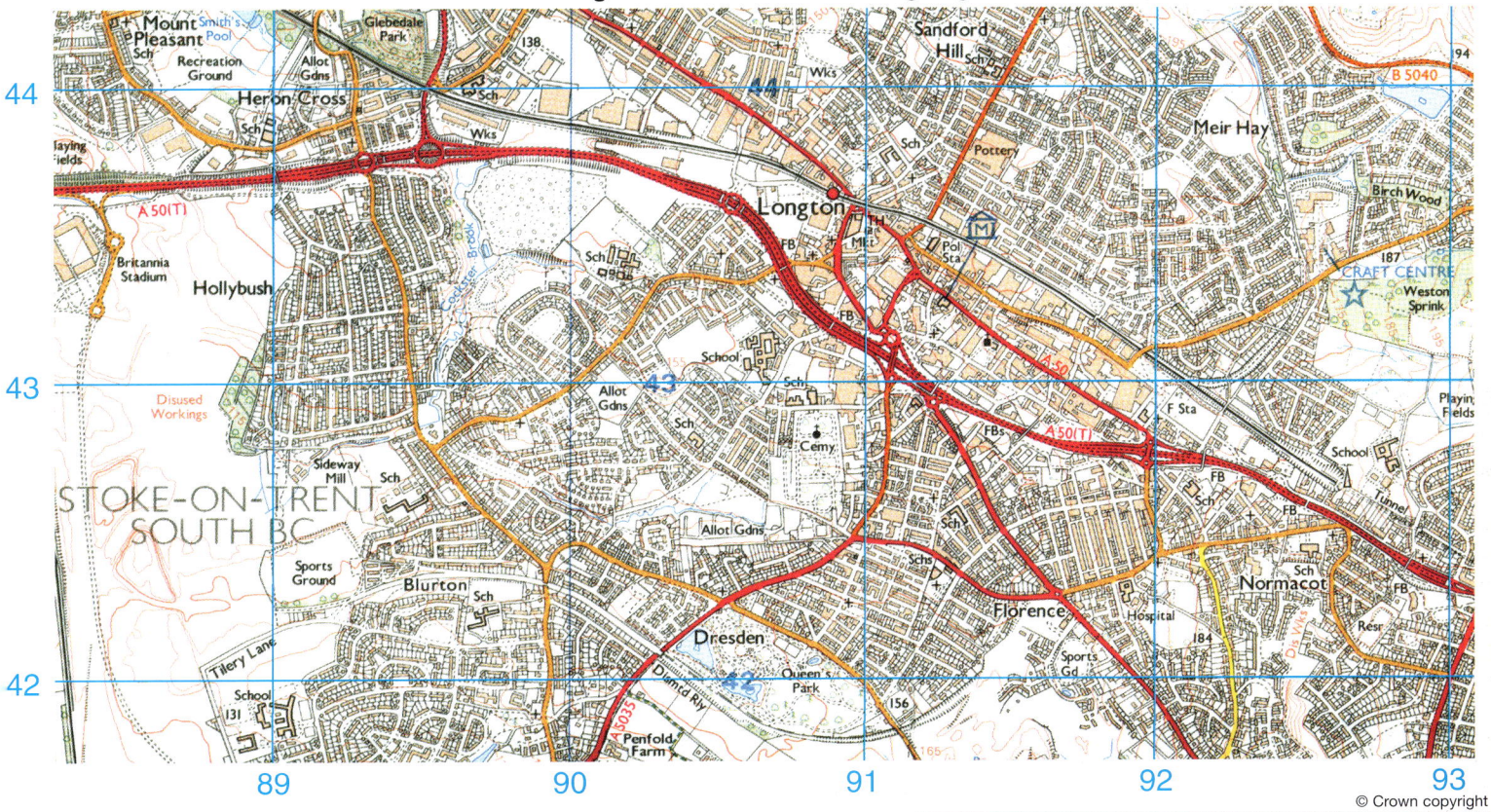

© Crown copyright

2 Development: Change in Contrasting Localities 35

Is this development of a local area?
Obuasi, Ashanti Goldfield, Ghana

› Where?
The gold operation at Obuasi is 200 km northwest of Accra in Ghana. It is in the Ashanti region whose centre is Kumasi.

› What?
The Ashanti Goldfields Company (AGC) owns the Obuasi gold mine. AGC was established in London in 1897. This company is now a Plc, with the Ghanaian government having a stake of about 20%. Gold is a scarce resource; even where it is found, there is usually only 3 or 4 grams per ton of rock, and is very expensive to extract. The metal is soft and attractive and makes good jewelry. Ingots of gold are used as reserves of 'money' that will not lose its value. However in Ghana, operations such as those at Obuasi were causing massive environmental destruction.

› Why?
Before the 1980s the gold mines around Obuasi were thought to be an environmental disaster. The atmosphere was polluted with arsenic, sulphur and dust. Vegetation had been killed by emissions from the roasting process. Ponds

△ **Figure 2.25** Overview of the Obusai mine, Central Ghana

behind dams contained poisonous material from the past and safe inert materials more recently. The landscape was scarred by open cast mining. The water was polluted by cyanide from modern processes. Fish were dead or poisonous, though the water was clear again 30 km downstream. Villagers had their water supply poisoned.

› When?
Since the 1990s AGC has had a sound environmental policy.

› How?
A new £5 million plant was opened in the early 1990s to extract the arsenic used in the gold extraction process. It has also built laboratories which enable the monitoring of workers' health and of the local air and water quality. **Tube wells** have been sunk for villagers to provide clean water supplies. AGC has also introduced safety at work policies; for example, dust monitoring which has reduced accidents from 150 to 30 a week. It has also helped with the local facilities; for example, schools and market stalls, street lighting, landfill sites for rubbish, water for dampening down dust.

◁ **Figure 2.26** A truck at Ashanti Goldfields

36 INVESTIGATING GEOGRAPHY A

FACT FILE: THE ASHANTI GOLD MINES

Estimates suggest that there is at least 20 million ounces of gold available to be mined at Obuasi.

Ashanti gold mine's production rate puts it in the world's top ten.

Ashanti has been mining in Ghana for more than a century.

Gold output from Obuasi is between 550 000 and 650 000 oz per year. The cash cost of production is US$223/oz (1999).

Within the Obuasi township AGC has provided 15 boreholes with handpumps to improve water supply.

In 1999, 743 111 oz of gold were produced in Obuasi.

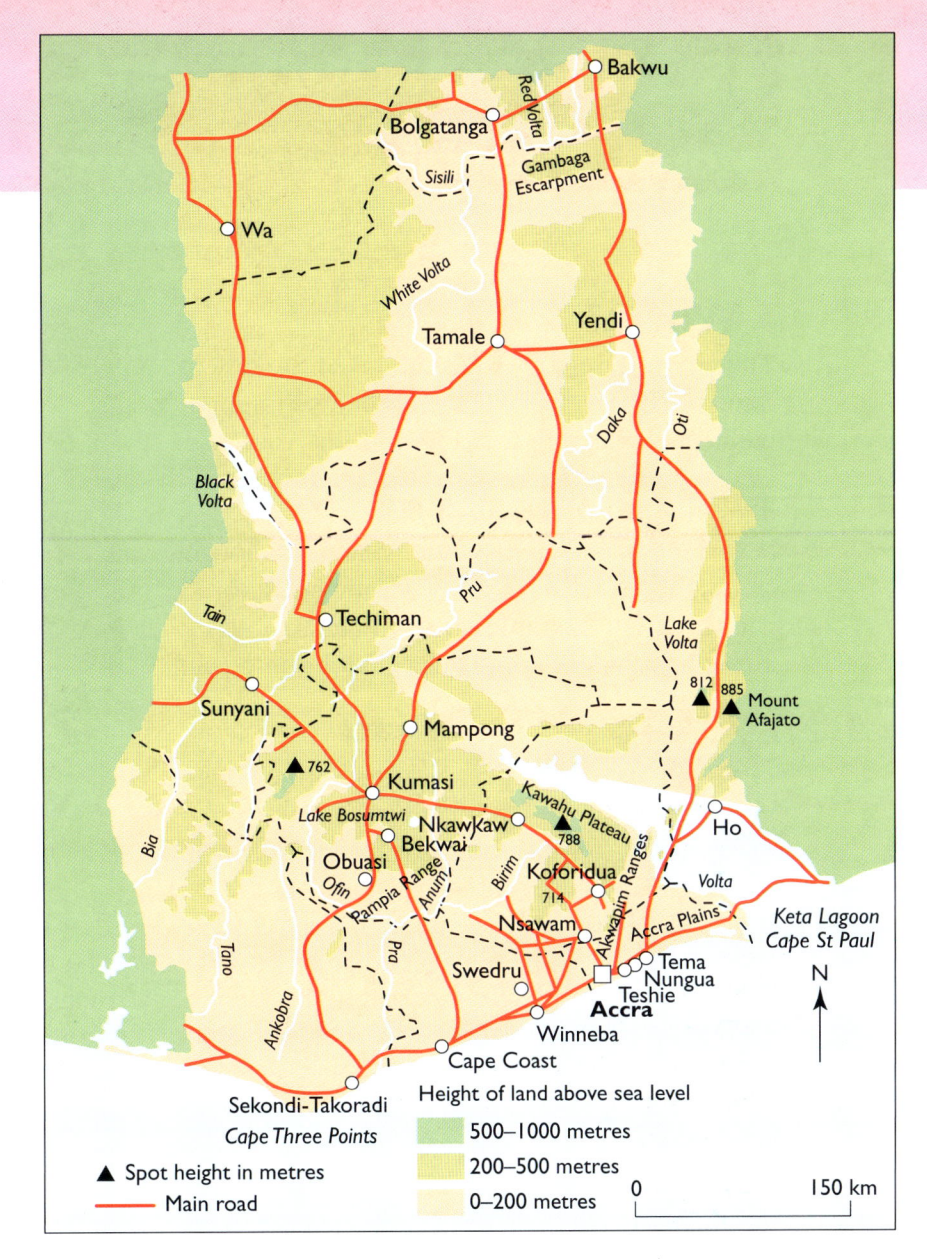

ICT links

Some useful websites are:

www.ashanti.com

www.mining-technology.com/projects/Obuasi/index.html

www.moles.org/Project Underground/reports/goldpack/goldpack_f.html

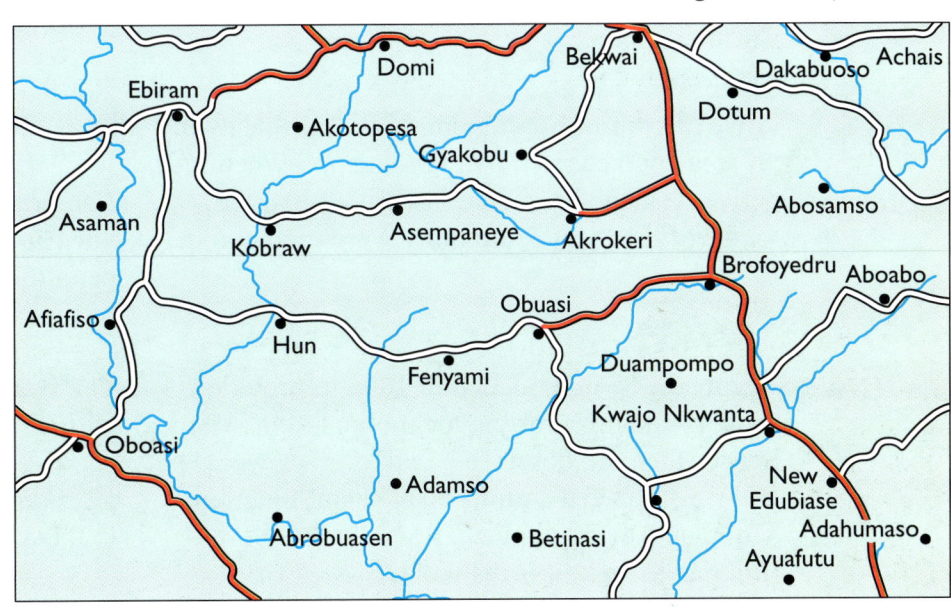

▲ Figure 2.27 Map of Ghana

▲ Figure 2.28 Map showing Obuasi

2 Development: Change in Contrasting Localities

Is this development of a local area?

Nordbad Swimming Pool, Ausere, Germany

› Where?

The city of Dresden is the capital of Saxony in South East Germany. The Nordbad swimming baths are located in the centre of the Ausere Neustadt (outer new town). It is characterised by poorly-equipped **tenement blocks**. At the beginning of the 1990s, over 65% of its housing stock did not have a bath or a shower. Before **reunification** unemployment in the area was 20% and many buildings were falling into ruin.

△ **Figure 2.30** Solar roof-top collectors on buildings surrounding the Nordbad

› What?

The Nordbad project was funded by the European Regional Development fund aimed to stimulate urban regeneration in Dresden's inner city district of Ausere. By renovating the 19th century swimming baths, the project acted as a magnet for other redevelopments in the area.

△ **Figure 2.29** Nordbad swimming pool in operation, 1997

By upgrading the **neighbourhood** and providing training opportunities for unemployed people, the project helped to improve the local **economy** and to provide a boost to house values.

The project has also managed to create a new sense of **community** amongst local residents in an area characterised by high unemployment. An active residents' association ensured that the views of the local community were included in the project.

› Why?

Nordbad was first opened in 1896 to provide sanitary facilities for the local population. Many houses then did not have a bath or a shower. The baths also played an important social function, acting as a meeting place. It gradually fell into ruin due to lack of investment.

› When?

The project took place in the mid-late 1990s.

› How?

The Nordbad is located in the heart of a street block, which had made **pedestrian** access to the baths difficult. As one part of the project, a number of the surrounding buildings were demolished, opening up the Nordbad to pedestrian access. To further improve the area around the baths, a number of other buildings and their surroundings were developed. A children's playground was built, and benches, a fountain area, a sun bathing lawn, and plants were introduced. The aim was to make the whole Nordbad complex a centre for health, social and recreational activities for the community.

The project also provided opportunities for **vocational** training for young unemployed people in specialist building skills related to the restoration of listed buildings.

The Nordbad re-opened with a swimming pool, with an adjustable floor for variable water depths, a children's paddling pool, sauna, physiotherapy units and cleansing baths. Schools in the area use the pool for lessons.

FACT FILE: THE NORDBAD SWIMMING BATHS

The Nordbad now provides bathing for the 12 000 local residents and the rest of the city.

During the first half of 1997, 30 000 people visited the baths.

The 24 companies employed to undertake restoration work were obliged to employ and train young unemployed people.

37 unemployed people were given jobs.

17 trainees gained building qualifications.

20% of all housing in the area has been modified.

△ **Figure 2.31** Map of Germany

ICT links

A useful website:
www.inforegio.org/urban/upp/src.Bullet08.htm

△ **Figure 2.32** Aerial view of area surrounding Nordbad

2 Development: Change in Contrasting Localities 39

Assessment tasks

Whenever we study a place in geography, it is always hard to discover the full story. Any place studied at whatever scale is unique. There is nowhere the same as the place that you live. There is nowhere else the same as Ausere, Obuasi or Stoke. The developments that you have investigated in those places are only a small part of what those places are like. Many people live and work in those places and because of their different experiences and values will have different views about the same place. You have found out about specific changes that have taken place there, but there are also other events happening in those places.

A search on the Internet revealed three different events happening in Dresden, Stoke and Obuasi.

So is this the full story?

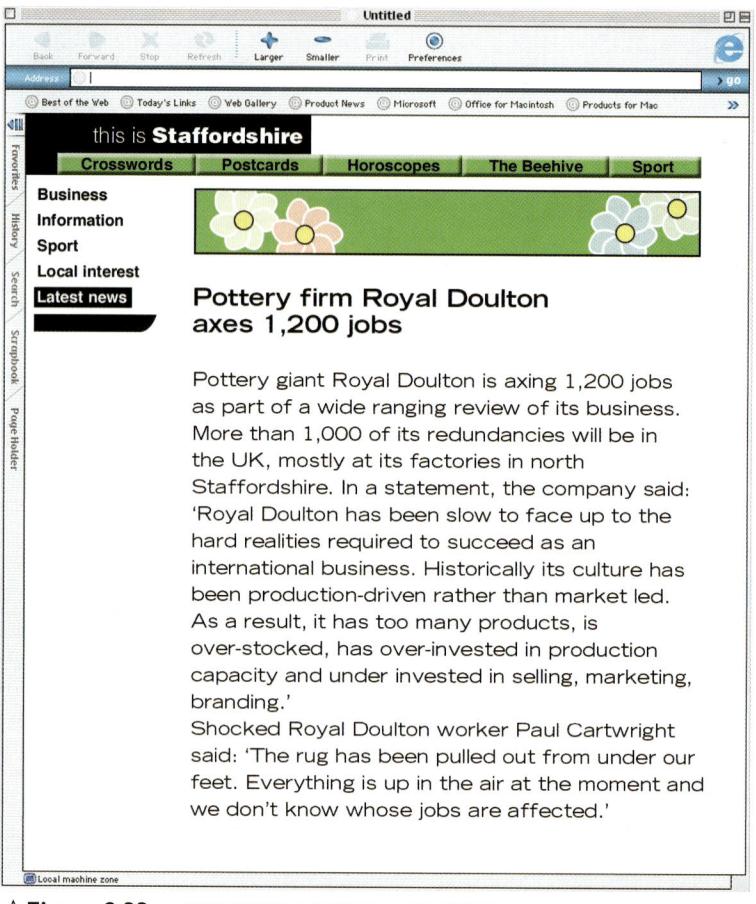

Pottery firm Royal Doulton axes 1,200 jobs

Pottery giant Royal Doulton is axing 1,200 jobs as part of a wide ranging review of its business. More than 1,000 of its redundancies will be in the UK, mostly at its factories in north Staffordshire. In a statement, the company said: 'Royal Doulton has been slow to face up to the hard realities required to succeed as an international business. Historically its culture has been production-driven rather than market led. As a result, it has too many products, is over-stocked, has over-invested in production capacity and under invested in selling, marketing, branding.'
Shocked Royal Doulton worker Paul Cartwright said: 'The rug has been pulled out from under our feet. Everything is up in the air at the moment and we don't know whose jobs are affected.'

△ Figure 2.33

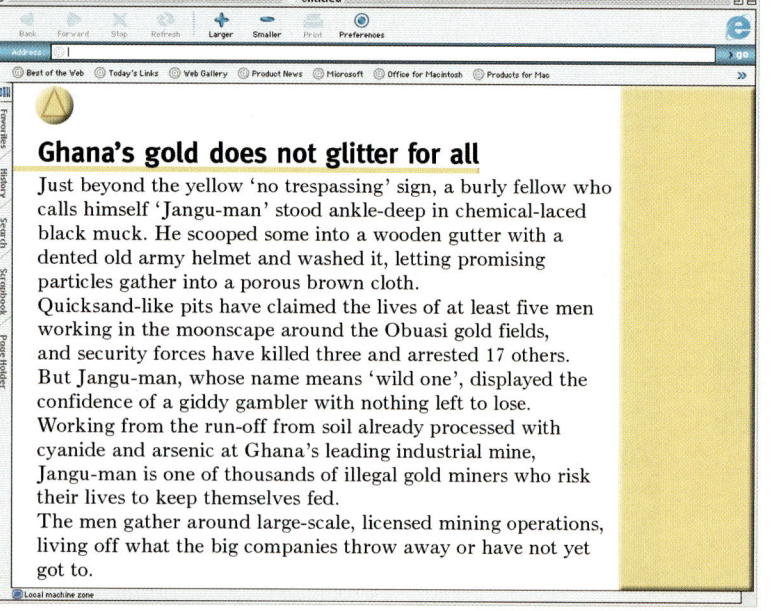

Ghana's gold does not glitter for all

Just beyond the yellow 'no trespassing' sign, a burly fellow who calls himself 'Jangu-man' stood ankle-deep in chemical-laced black muck. He scooped some into a wooden gutter with a dented old army helmet and washed it, letting promising particles gather into a porous brown cloth.
Quicksand-like pits have claimed the lives of at least five men working in the moonscape around the Obuasi gold fields, and security forces have killed three and arrested 17 others. But Jangu-man, whose name means 'wild one', displayed the confidence of a giddy gambler with nothing left to lose. Working from the run-off from soil already processed with cyanide and arsenic at Ghana's leading industrial mine, Jangu-man is one of thousands of illegal gold miners who risk their lives to keep themselves fed.
The men gather around large-scale, licensed mining operations, living off what the big companies throw away or have not yet got to.

△ Figure 2.34

German women create their jobs by starting their own businesses

DRESDEN, GERMANY – Viola Winkler is a woman on the go. Ms Winkler is head of the Saxony Training Institute in Dresden, Germany, which trains prospective entrepreneurs in managerial, marketing, and other business skills. When an important call comes in, she springs from the table and darts for her office.
A lot of other eastern German women would like to follow in her tracks. One-third of east German businesses are owned by women, compared with one-fourth to one-fifth in western Germany, according to the Federal Labour Bureau. Women head 150,000 firms employing roughly 1 million people, at a time when German unemployment stands above 4.8 million, at near record levels. One reason many east German women have become entrepreneurs is that they were laid off following German reunification in 1990. 'Women were the first to be removed from the workforce' Winkler says, 'as waves of unprofitable, uncompetitive Communist-era factories were shut down between 1990 and 1995 1.6 million women lost their jobs, compared with 1.2 million men...'

Figure 2.35 ▷

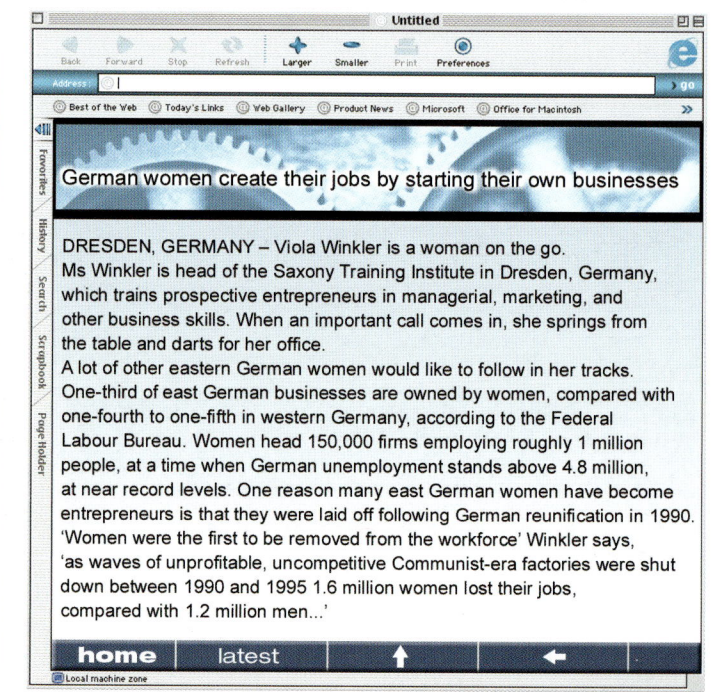

Target tasks

1 Look back at the shorthand definition of development on page 26. What do you understand by the terms: Choices, Quality of Life and Values. Use page 27 to help you with Choices, page 28 to help you with Quality of Life and page 30 to help you with Values.

Development Terms	I think this means	For example	I also think it means	For example	Finally I think.....
Quality of Life					
Choices					
Values					

2 Would you say that the Ceramic Quarter project (pages 34 and 35) has helped people in that area to improve their choices, and quality of life? What do you think were the aims (values) of the project?

The Ceramic Quarter Project	I think has improved	For example	I also think it has improved	For example	Finally I think.....
Quality of Life					
Choices					
Values					

3 Read the Internet article opposite (Figure 2.33). Use the futures frames on page 42 to describe Paul Cartwright's current position, what he might think his future position could be and what he thinks his future probably will be. By the future in this case we mean the next 10 years. Look at the example of a futures frame for 'Jangu-man' on page 42 to help you.

4 To make Paul Cartwright's preferred future into his probable future, what actions would need to be taken?

5 Describe a possible development project that could improve Paul Cartwright's quality of life, using the headings, Where?, What?, Why?, When?, How?.

2 Development: Change in Contrasting Localities

Assessment tasks

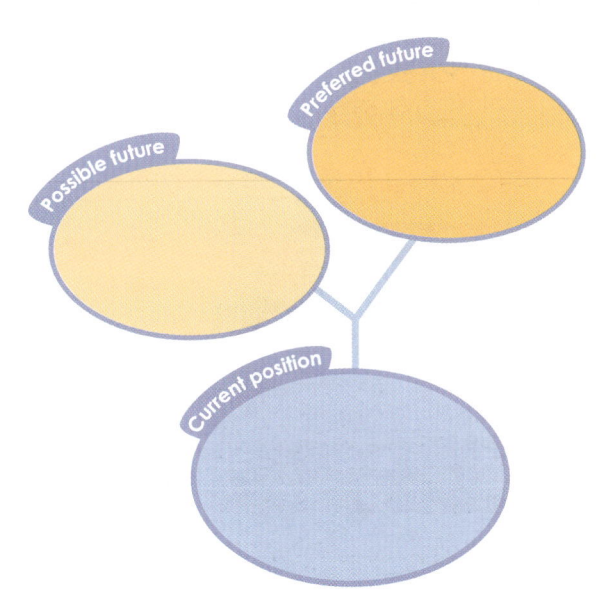

Figure 2.36 Futures frame

Possible future / Preferred future / Current position (empty frame)

Figure 2.37 Future frame for 'Jangu-man'

Possible future
> Becomes ill from working in unhealthy atmosphere
> Sees friends die
> Continues to work illegally
> Has very little money
> Continues to see others become very wealthy from gold

Preferred future
> Has a secure job
> Has health care
> Has a home
> Is able to afford to buy food
> Can live safely without the threat of violence

Current position
> No job
> Little money
> Putting health at risk
> Living in violent atmosphere
> Working illegally to feed himself
> Working in an area poisoned with cyanide and arsenic
> Sees others who are becoming wealthy from the mine

Extension Tasks

1 Using the Internet information (Figure 2.35) to help you, draw and complete a futures frame for an unemployed woman in Dresden. You may wish to refer to the example above (Figure 2.37). Use three colours for the information on your frame: one for facts, one for opinions, and one for statistical data.

2 Using the information on pages 36 and 37 for Obuasi, can you suggest a development project that could improve Jangu-man's quality of life? You might like to use the frame below to help you.

Development Project	The project would improve things for.....by	For example	I also think it would improve because...	For example	Finally I think....
Quality of Life					
Choices					
Values					

3 Now do the same for the lady in Dresden, using the information from pages 38 and 39 as a reference.

4 Which of your two development projects do you think will be the most successful? Can you explain why?

42 INVESTIGATING GEOGRAPHY A

Review

So how have you developed?

Activities

Figure 2.38 Environmental water sampling at Obuasi

1 Look back at the concept maps that you produced at the start of the unit. This was how you answered question 1 on page 24. Either draw new concept maps to show what you now know, or in a different colour add to your originals.

What surprises you, or interests you about what you have learnt?

2 Look at the photo (above) and the annotated sketch (below). Using these as a guide, choose one of the photos from page 25. Draw an outline sketch of the photo and annotate to show what you now know about that place.

Figure 2.39 Annotated sketch of water sampling at Obuasi

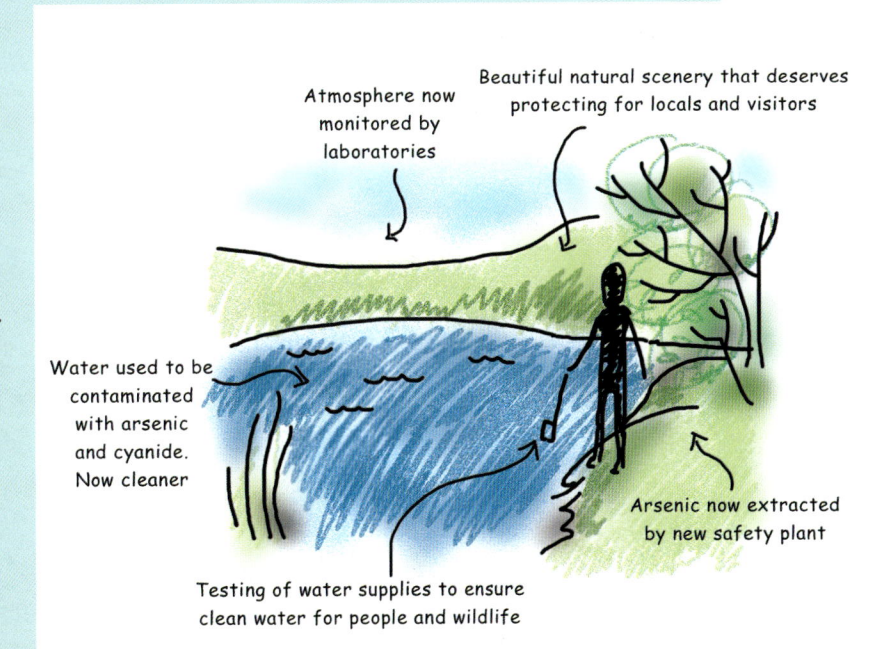

- Atmosphere now monitored by laboratories
- Beautiful natural scenery that deserves protecting for locals and visitors
- Water used to be contaminated with arsenic and cyanide. Now cleaner
- Arsenic now extracted by new safety plant
- Testing of water supplies to ensure clean water for people and wildlife

3 How do you remember learning during this section of work? Make a list of the skills that you think that you have used. Underline any that you think are geography specific. Underline in a different colour any that you think that you might use again.

4 Choose a development project that has happened in your own local area. You might like to investigate it to see if you can produce information like that on pages 34 and 35. This will enable you to transfer what you have learnt about development to a new area.

5 Would you like to add to or alter the shorthand definition of development on page 26?

2 Development: Change in Contrasting Localities

3 Weather and Climate

How are images of the weather described in books?

I have respect for the Danish winter. The cold – not what is measured on a thermometer, but what you can actually feel – depends more on the force of the wind and the relative humidity in the air than on the actual temperature... When the first clammy rain showers begin slapping me and November in the face with a wet towel, I meet them with fur-lined capucines, black alpaca leggings, a long Scottish skirt, a sweater and a black waterproof cape.

◁ From **Miss Smilla's Feeling for Snow** by Peter Hoeg

Figure 3.1 Images of weather from fiction

This morning when I set off it was −19°F (−28°C)... Unless you have a particularly vivid imagination, or are reading this in a chest freezer, you may find such extreme chilliness difficult to conceive... When you step outside in such weather, for the first instant it is startlingly invigorating – not unlike the experience of diving into cold water... Your face feels as it would after a sharp slap, your extremities are aching and every breath you take hurts.

△ From **Notes from a Big Country** by Bill Bryson

Gusts of wind buffeted the truck as we pulled to a stop... We put up our tent as quickly as possible, but even with the tent, refuge eluded us that night. For hours we lay in our sleeping bags listening to the wind. Whirling through the pass... it roared like traffic on a distant freeway as it rushed towards the dunes... Gravel rasped across the ground cloth, and sand sifted through the mosquito netting. Morning finally came but brought no respite from the wind, which still blew cold and steady from the south east.

◁ From **Seasons of the Wind** by Janice Bowers

Activities

1 Which book would you most like to read? Give reasons for your choice.

2 Using this favourite extract, imagine you are the author and write a short paragraph to describe what happens next.

3 Imagine you work for a publishing house, like Hodder & Stoughton. Design a front cover for each of the three books, to show the images described by the writers.

How does the weather affect me and you?

Weather means the day-to-day changes in the **atmosphere** for a particular place, e.g. temperature, **precipitation**, wind speed. **Climate** means the average of the weather conditions for a particular area.

Does the weather affect me in the playground?

△ **Figure 3.2** Calendar

△ **Figure 3.3** Playground

Activities

4 In which month are you most likely to:-

- eat ice cream
- kick leaves as you walk along the pavement
- be off school with the flu
- wear wellington boots
- throw snowballs at a friend
- play in the back garden
- wear sun-tan cream
- wear hat and gloves
- dry clothes on a washing line
- have a picnic
- scrape ice off the car windscreen
- see "fog Ahead" signs on the motorway
- wear shorts
- take an umbrella with you.

5 From your own knowledge at school or using Figure 3.3, discuss in pairs where you would place the following and give reasons for your choice.

- benches for pupils to sit in the sun
- trees to give shelter from the wind
- benches for pupils who want to sit in the shade
- a washing line to dry the art aprons
- a greenhouse to grow tomatoes.

3 Weather and Climate

How does the weather affect me and you?

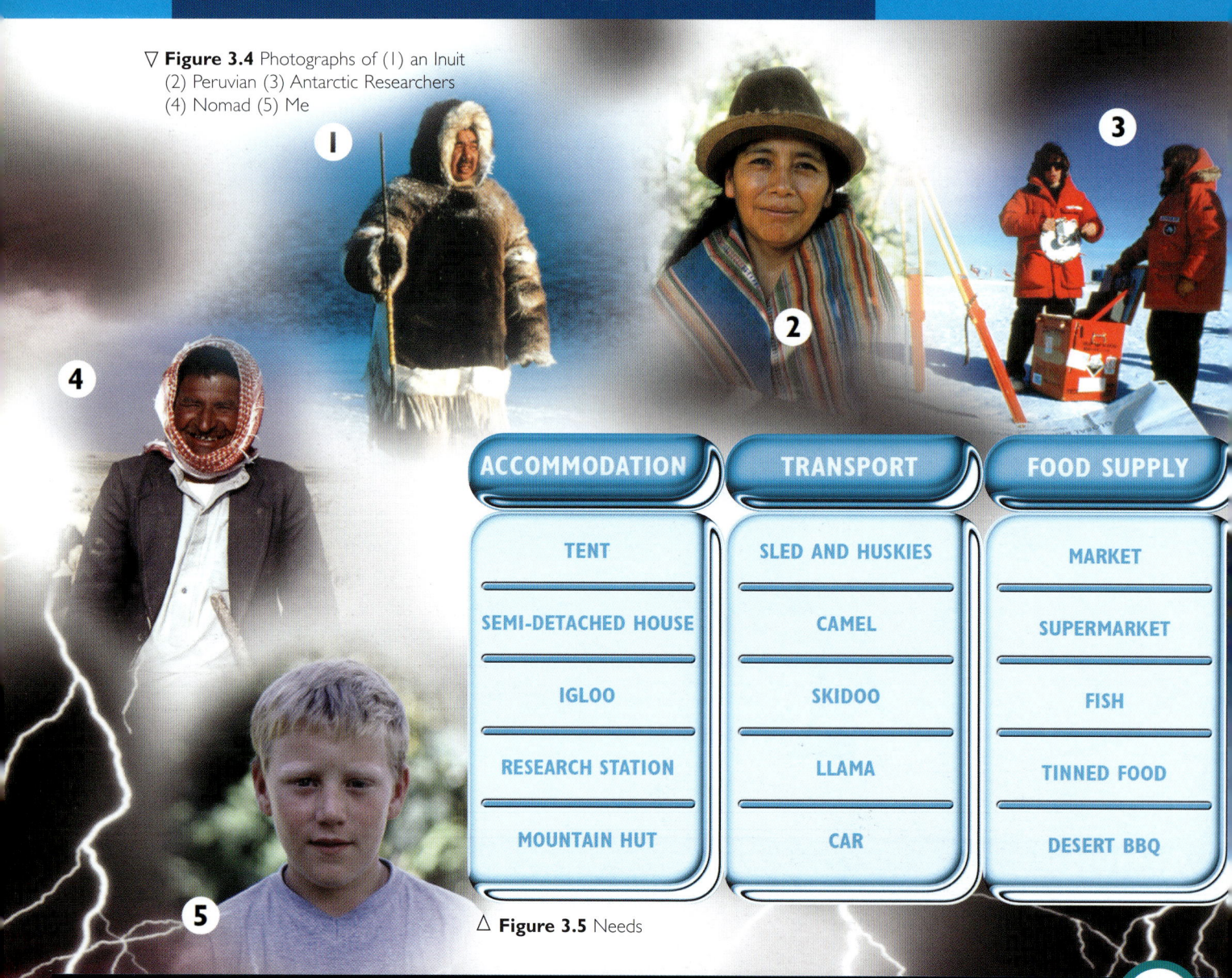

Figure 3.4 Photographs of (1) an Inuit (2) Peruvian (3) Antarctic Researchers (4) Nomad (5) Me

Figure 3.5 Needs

ACCOMMODATION
- TENT
- SEMI-DETACHED HOUSE
- IGLOO
- RESEARCH STATION
- MOUNTAIN HUT

TRANSPORT
- SLED AND HUSKIES
- CAMEL
- SKIDOO
- LLAMA
- CAR

FOOD SUPPLY
- MARKET
- SUPERMARKET
- FISH
- TINNED FOOD
- DESERT BBQ

Activities

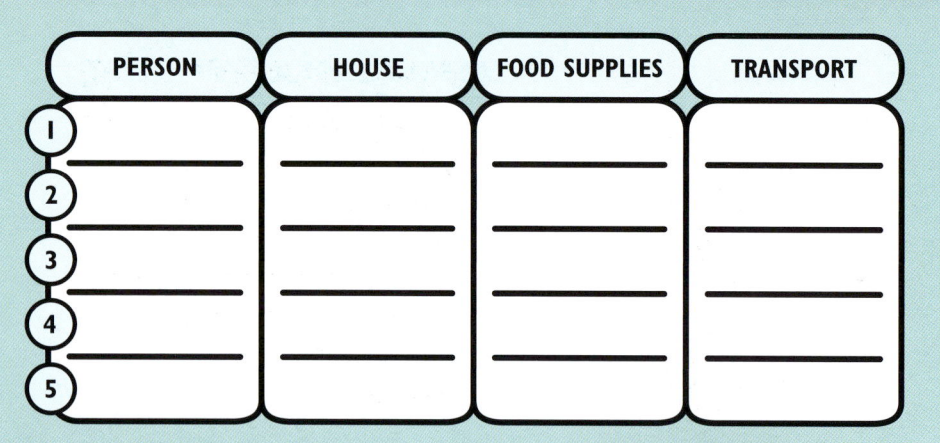

PERSON	HOUSE	FOOD SUPPLIES	TRANSPORT
1			
2			
3			
4			
5			

Figure 3.6 Choices table

1 Copy out the table, Figure 3.6, and then match up each person with the house, food and transport they are most likely to have.

2 Explain how you made your choices.

46 INVESTIGATING GEOGRAPHY A

Who needs to know what tomorrow's weather will be? Why?

> We need time to grit the roads overnight before the ice or snow settles. We need to keep the roads clear for people travelling to work and school the next day.

> Frost and rain can affect the setting of mortar and cement.

> I clean as many windows as I can when it is dry. I can go weeks without earning money if there are a lot of downpours.

> We use radar to predict how long showers are going to last. If the rain is prolonged it is worth putting the covers on the court and disrupting the players.

Some people are paid to measure and record weather – they are called **meteorologists**. The term meteorologist comes from the ancient Greek term *meteor* or 'things in the air'. Meteorologists can work for many employers, including:
- the government
- universities
- television and radio stations
- nuclear power plants
- airports
- farms and fisheries
- insurance and investment companies.

△ **Figure 3.7** Why I need to know about the weather

Activities

3 Read through the ways weather affects people's jobs. Write down ways in which the following people might be affected by the weather:
- fire fighter
- ice cream seller
- farmer.

3 Weather and Climate

How do we measure and record weather?

▽ **Figure 3.8** Weather instruments

Activities

1 Match the pictures with the following descriptions:

- With this piece of equipment we can measure the coldest temperatures during 24 hours and the warmest temperatures.

- A metal container that collects rainwater that falls into the funnel at the top of the cylinder. At the end of each 24-hour period the water is tipped out into a measuring cylinder and the number of millimetres (mm) are recorded.

- A piece of equipment which has cups that are caught by the wind and rotated. As the cups spin, their speed will be shown on the scale.

- This equipment provides protection for the measuring instruments. It has vents to allow air to circulate inside.

- This piece of equipment may look like a clock but its dial moves according to the weight of the air.

2 Choose the correct name for each picture using the following list:

a **Wind vane**
b **Barometer**
c **Rain gauge**
d **Anemometer**
e **Minimum-maximum thermometer**
f **Stevenson screen**

3 Draw the piece of equipment which was not described in question **1** and add your own description.

48 INVESTIGATING GEOGRAPHY A

The Meteorological Office

The International Meteorological Organisation (IMO) was established in 1878 to monitor and share weather records. The IMO helped people in many different aspects of life, such as farming, flying and sailing. After World War Two, the IMO was re-named the World Meteorological Organisation (WMO). The WMO regulate weather monitoring and forecasting around the world. In December 1951 the WMO was recognised by the United Nations as a specialised agency due to its importance in people's lives.

In the UK, the Met Office dates back to 1854. In the early days it provided a service to the shipping industry, warning of wind conditions and sea currents.

The 21st century Met Office is divided into six units. Over 2 000 people work for the Met Office, at over 80 locations in the UK and overseas.

▽ **Figure 3.9** The work of the Met Office

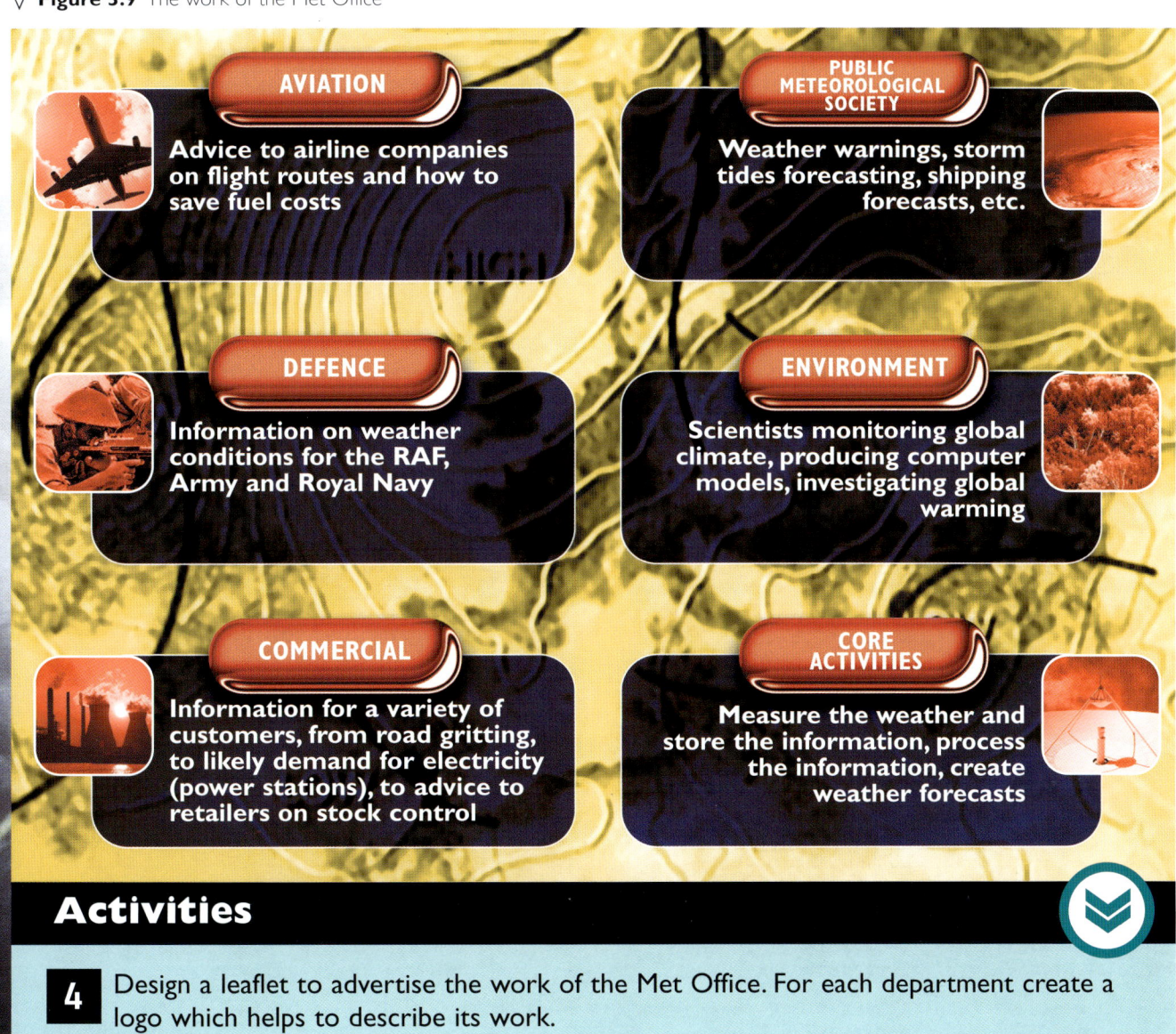

AVIATION
Advice to airline companies on flight routes and how to save fuel costs

PUBLIC METEOROLOGICAL SOCIETY
Weather warnings, storm tides forecasting, shipping forecasts, etc.

DEFENCE
Information on weather conditions for the RAF, Army and Royal Navy

ENVIRONMENT
Scientists monitoring global climate, producing computer models, investigating global warming

COMMERCIAL
Information for a variety of customers, from road gritting, to likely demand for electricity (power stations), to advice to retailers on stock control

CORE ACTIVITIES
Measure the weather and store the information, process the information, create weather forecasts

Activities

4 Design a leaflet to advertise the work of the Met Office. For each department create a logo which helps to describe its work.

3 Weather and Climate

How do we measure and record weather?

Weather maps

Weather maps are used to show temperature, precipitation, wind speed, wind direction and cloud cover. The special symbols used to show the information on a weather map are called the **synoptic code**. Figure 3.10 shows the weather conditions for most of Europe on one day in July.

Some weather maps show the information recorded at individual weather stations. The weather stations are represented by a circle. The synoptic symbols (Figure 3.11) are used to show information for each station. In Figure 3.12, the wind is blowing from the north-east at speeds of between 23 and 27 knots. The sky is 7/8 covered by cloud. Rain is falling. The temperature is 4°C.

▽ **Figure 3.10** A weather map for the UK on the 31st July 2000 (Information supplied by the Met Office)

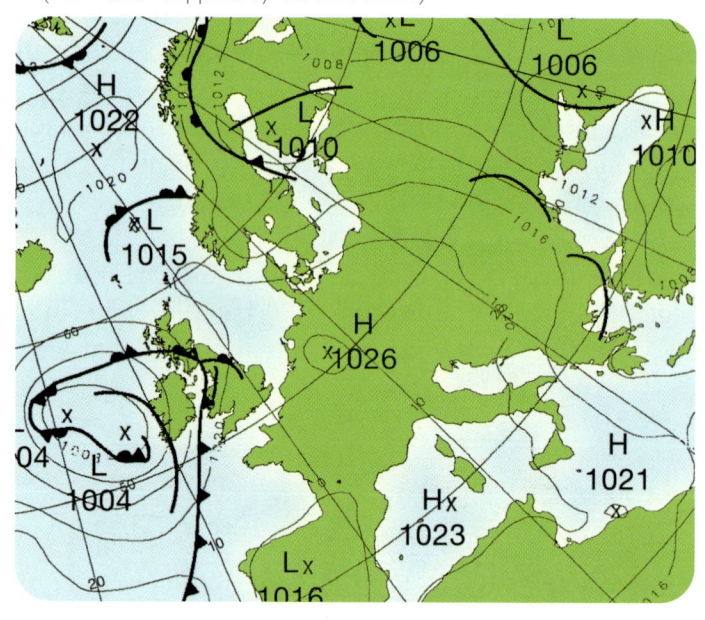

◁▷▽ Synoptic Symbols

▽ **Figure 3.11** The synoptic code (Information supplied by the Met Office)

WIND

Speed (knots)	Symbol	Speed (knots)	Symbol
Less than 1	⊚	33-37	
1-2		38-42	
3-7		43-47	
8-12		48-52	
13-17		53-57	
18-22		58-62	
23-27		98-102	
28-32		103-107	

The arrow from the weather station symbol shows the direction from which the wind is blowing. A system of feathers' is used to show wind speeds; full feathers are used for 10 knots and half feathers for 5 knots. Pennants (like flags) are used for wind speeds of 50 knots.

PRECIPITATION

	Symbol		Symbol
Rain	●	Fog	≡
Drizzle	❵	Thunderstorm	↙
Shower	▽	Hail	▲
Snow	✳		

TEMPERATURE
This is given in degrees Celsius. It is plotted to the left of the weather station symbol and above any weather symbols.

50 INVESTIGATING GEOGRAPHY A

▽ **Figure 3.12** A weather station

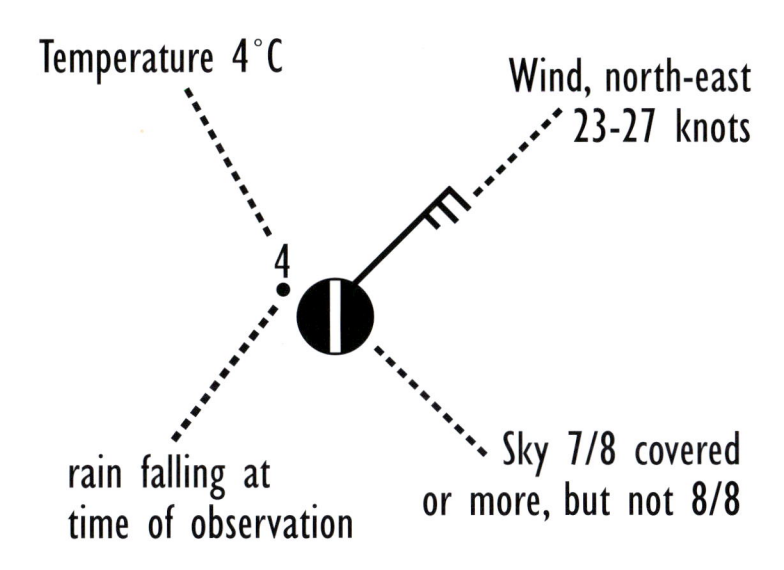

Temperature 4°C

Wind, north-east 23–27 knots

4

rain falling at time of observation

Sky 7/8 covered or more, but not 8/8

CLOUD COVER

	Symbol		Symbol
Clear sky	○	5/8 covered	◐
covered 1/8 or less, but not zero	⊙	6/8 covered	◐
2/8 covered	◔	7/8 covered	◕
3/8 covered	◔	sky completely covered	●
4/8 covered	◑	sky obscured e.g. by fog	⊗

Activities

1 Using the information about the synoptic code, describe the weather conditions for each set of symbols in Figure 3.13.

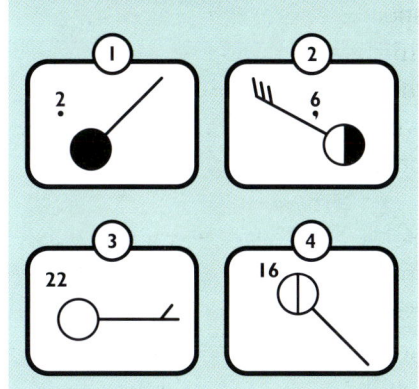

△ **Figure 3.13** Weather stations

2 Draw the symbols you would use to show the following weather conditions:

a Wind from the north; speed 48–52 knots. Temperature 3°C. Hail is falling and the sky 5/8 covered by cloud.

b Wind from the south-east; speed less than 1 knot. Temperature 27°C. No precipitation and clear skies.

c Wind from the north-west; speed 23–27 knots. Temperature 10°C. Rain is falling. Sky is obscured by fog.

3 Cut out of a newspaper a local or UK weather map. Describe the weather shown on that day.

3 Weather and Climate 51

How do we predict the weather?

People have been measuring the weather for over 2 000 years. There are records from the 17th century showing scientists and amateurs making local studies of temperature and **air pressure**. It was not until 1853 that weather was recorded on an international co-ordinated scale to help sailors. Even today, one of the most accurate weather forecasts available is the Shipping Forecast.

◁ **Figure 3.14** Shipping Forecast areas

△ **Figure 3.15** Shipping Forecast 14 July 2001 (Information supplied by the Met Office)

NOW THE SHIPPING FORECAST ISSUED BY THE MET. OFFICE AT 11.30 ON SATURDAY 14 JULY 2001 THE AREA FORECASTS FOR THE NEXT 24 HOURS

SOUTH UTSIRE
VARIABLE 3 BECOMING NORTHERLY 4. SHOWERS. GOOD

FORTIES
NORTHEASTERLY BACKING NORTHWESTERLY 3 OR 4, OCCASIONALLY 5. RAIN OR SHOWERS. MODERATE OR GOOD

CROMARTY FORTH TYNE
NORTHEASTERLY BACKING NORTHWESTERLY 3 OR 4, OCCASIONALLY 5 AT FIRST IN TYNE. RAIN OR SHOWERS. MODERATE OR GOOD

HUMBER
VARIABLE 3 BECOMING WESTERLY 4 OCCASIONALLY 5. SHOWERS. GOOD

THAMES DOVER
SOUTHWESTERLY, VEERING NORTHWESTERLY FOR A TIME, 3 OR 4. SHOWERS. GOOD

Activities

Foundation

'Dover: Mainly a southwesterly wind, will change to a northwesterly wind for a time, wind speed is 3 or 4 on the Beaufort scale, which is 12–28 km per hour so litter and hair will be blown about. There will be some showers.'

1 Imagine you are travelling on a ferry from Dover to Calais. You would sail through the Dover shipping area. Your journey would last about an hour. Describe the weather on your journey, using the information about Dover. Your description could be a diary entry or a picture.

Target

2 Imagine you are sailing on a cargo ship from the port of Kingston-upon-Hull to the port of Rotterdam. You will travel through two shipping areas: Humber and Thames (Figure 3.14). Use the shipping forecast to describe the weather you experience on your seven-hour journey, or draw a storyboard to show how the weather changes during your journey.

Extension

3 Imagine you are maintenance engineers based at Aberdeen. Your first journey is to visit oil rigs in the Forties shipping area (Figure 3.14). You will then return to Aberdeen before boarding a fishing vessel on an overnight journey from Aberdeen to Stavanger (Norway). Use the shipping forecast to describe the weather you experience on your journeys, or draw a storyboard to show how the weather changes during your journeys.

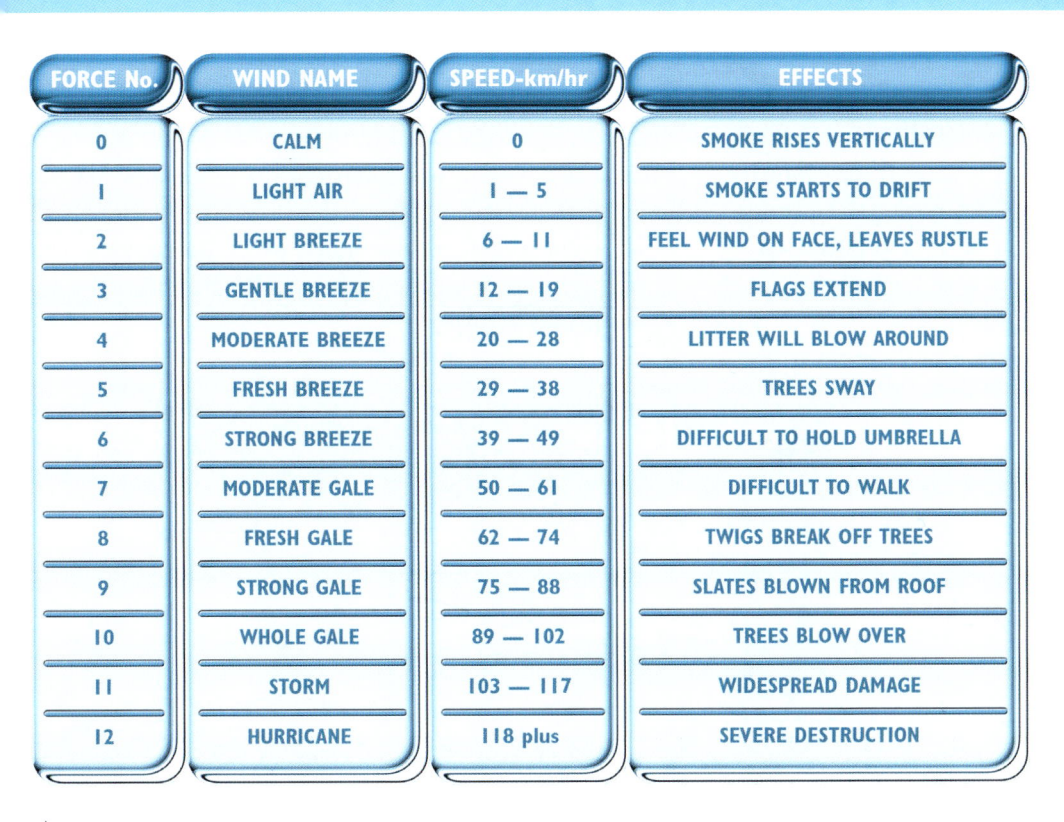

FORCE No.	WIND NAME	SPEED-km/hr	EFFECTS
0	CALM	0	SMOKE RISES VERTICALLY
1	LIGHT AIR	1 — 5	SMOKE STARTS TO DRIFT
2	LIGHT BREEZE	6 — 11	FEEL WIND ON FACE, LEAVES RUSTLE
3	GENTLE BREEZE	12 — 19	FLAGS EXTEND
4	MODERATE BREEZE	20 — 28	LITTER WILL BLOW AROUND
5	FRESH BREEZE	29 — 38	TREES SWAY
6	STRONG BREEZE	39 — 49	DIFFICULT TO HOLD UMBRELLA
7	MODERATE GALE	50 — 61	DIFFICULT TO WALK
8	FRESH GALE	62 — 74	TWIGS BREAK OFF TREES
9	STRONG GALE	75 — 88	SLATES BLOWN FROM ROOF
10	WHOLE GALE	89 — 102	TREES BLOW OVER
11	STORM	103 — 117	WIDESPREAD DAMAGE
12	HURRICANE	118 plus	SEVERE DESTRUCTION

△ **Figure 3.16** Beaufort wind scale

Wind direction can be plotted on a **wind rose** diagram (Figure 3.17). This helps us to identify patterns.

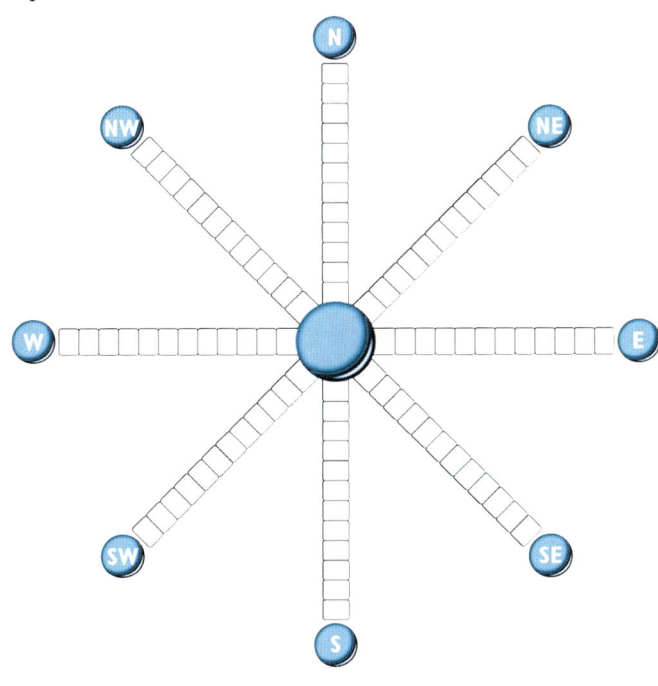

> Stages of drawing a Wind Rose

1. Draw an 8-point compass.
2. Label the 8 compass points.
3. Design a key for wind strength (force) using either colour or numbers.
4. For each windy day fill in a box on the correct compass axis.

△ **Figure 3.17** Wind rose diagram

DATE	DIRECTION	FORCE
1	WEST	2
2	WEST	3
3	SOUTH WEST	1
4	SOUTH WEST	1
5	SOUTH WEST	1
6		0
7		0
8	NORTH	3
9	NORTH	3
10	EAST	4
11	NORTH	5
12		0
13	WEST	1
14	SOUTH WEST	2
15	WEST	1
16		0
17	SOUTH EAST	2
18	SOUTH EAST	2
19	EAST	3
20	EAST	3
21	NORTH	3
22	NORTH	2
23	NORTH EAST	2
24	NORTH EAST	1
25		0
26		0
27		0
28	WEST	1
29	WEST	1
30	WEST	1

△ **Figure 3.18** Wind data

In the shipping forecast (Figure 3.15), wind direction and speed is mentioned many times. A school has collected the wind information for the month of April (Figure 3.18).

Activities

4 Have a go at drawing a wind rose by using information provided by your teacher, or the data for April in Figure 3.18.

3 Weather and Climate 53

Climate

The average weather conditions (climate) are worked out by studying all the weather records over a long time (usually 25 years). Knowing the climate of an area is very useful, for example plants will not grow if temperatures are below 6°C; this information helps farmers to plan their year.

Atlases show the main world climatic regions based on rainfall and temperature. Some atlas maps use a simple classification of five or six categories, with each climate shown by a different colour. Some maps use a more complicated system, such as 14 different colours or climate groups.

Activities

Using an atlas, find a world climate map.

1. How many different climate groups are shown?

2. What is the climate group for the UK?

3. How many climate groups are in a large country, like Australia?

Climate graphs

Geographers use **climate graphs** (Figures 3.19) to show the average monthly temperatures and rainfall for a particular place in a year. The temperature is shown by a line graph, which is drawn by joining together crosses. Each cross is placed in the middle of the space for each month and tells you the average temperature for that month. The rainfall is shown by a bar graph; each bar tells you the total rainfall for each month.

Activities

Study the climate graph, Figure 3.19, and then answer the following questions:

4. Which is the hottest month? What is its temperature?

5. Which is the coldest month? What is its temperature?

6. Which is the wettest month? How much rain fell in this month?

7. Which is the driest month? How much rain fell in this month?

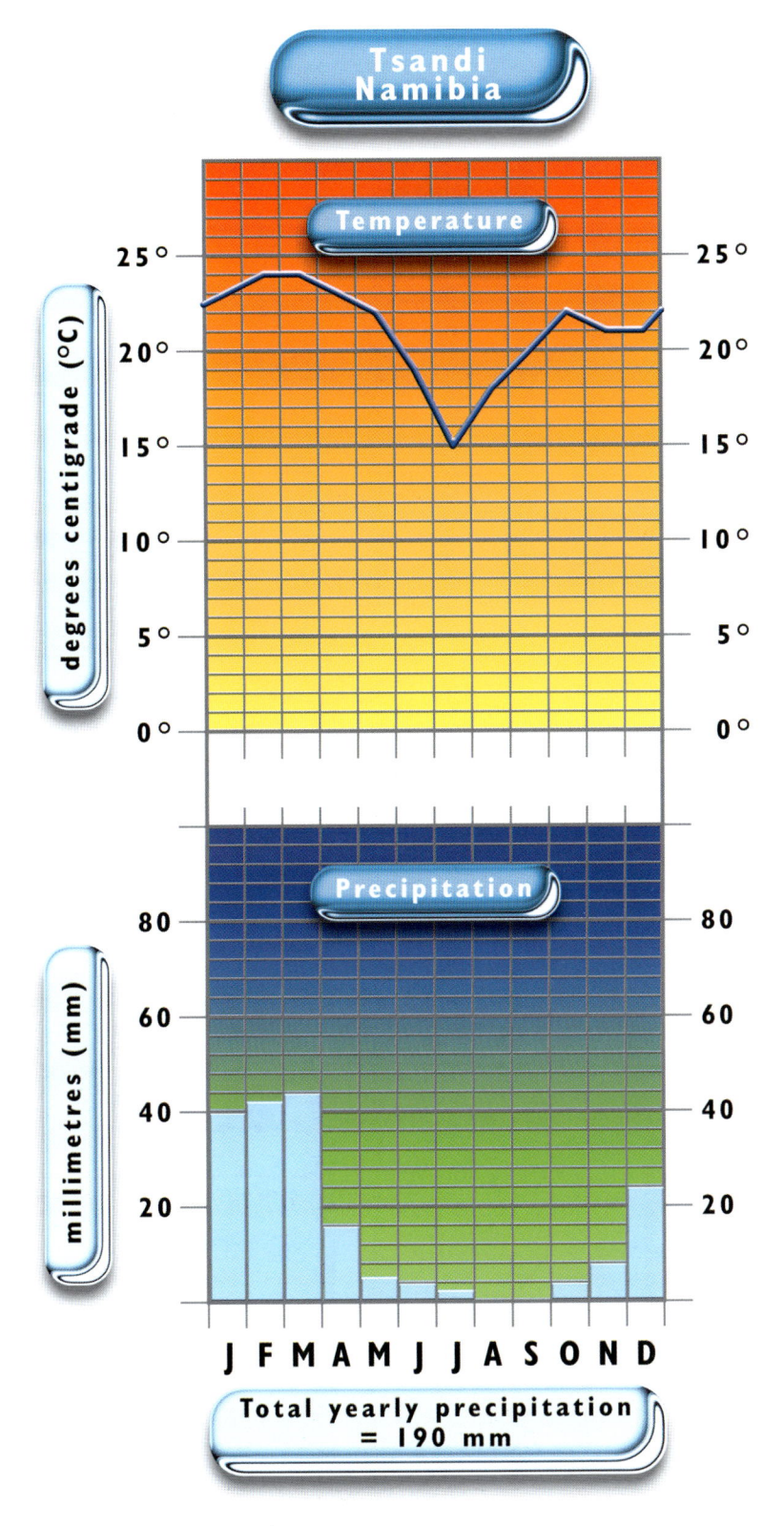

Figure 3.19 Climate graph for Tsandi in Namibia

Tsandi Namibia

Temperature

Precipitation

Total yearly precipitation = 190 mm

Activities

8 **Temperature range** tells a geographer how much the temperature changes during the year. It is worked out by taking the coldest temperature away from the hottest temperature. What is the temperature range for the climate graph of Tsandi?

9 For how many months of the year could plants grow in this area of Namibia? (The growing season is when temperatures are 6°C or above.)

10 Geographers do not calculate a rainfall range. It is useful to know the total annual rainfall, which is how much rain fell in the whole year. If the amount of rainfall for the whole year is less than 250 mm, the area is classed as a **desert**. What is the total annual rainfall for Tsandi? Is Tsandi in a desert area?

11 Why do temperatures in Tsandi fall during our summer time? (Look in an atlas.)

3 Weather and Climate

Climate
They've won the lottery!

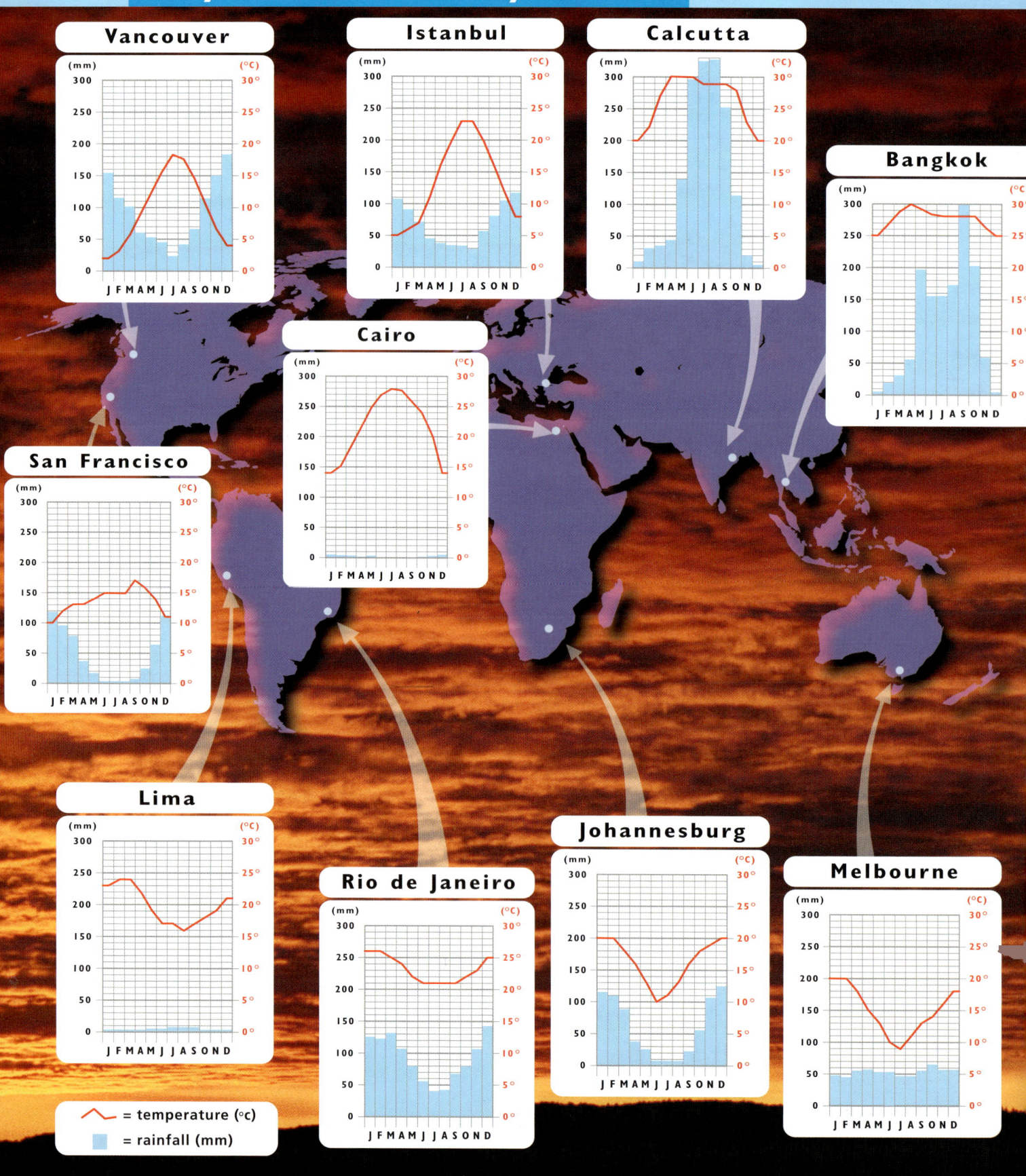

△ **Figure 3.20** World map

56 INVESTIGATING GEOGRAPHY A

MALARIA TABLETS
WATER BOTTLE
MONEY BELT
SUNGLASSES
SOCKS
CAMERA
SWISS ARMY KNIFE
SWIMSUIT/TRUNKS
PACK OF CARDS
DEODORANT
HAIR GEL/SPRAY
PERFUME/AFTERSHAVE
UNDERWEAR
UMBRELLA
SHIRT/BLOUSE
MOUNTAIN KIT
SARONG
SANDALS
MOSQUITO NET
SHORTS
T-SHIRT
THERMALS
MAKE UP BAG
BOOK
RAINCOAT
WASHING KIT (SOAP/TOOTHBRUSH)
SHEET & SLEEPING BAG
LONG SKIRT
TOWEL
JOGGING BOTTOMS
SUN-TAN LOTION
SHAMPOO & CONDITIONER
DRESS
SMART TROUSERS
HAIRDRYER
ROLL MAT
FLEECE
JEANS
SMART SHOES
JUMPER
TRAINERS
TRAVEL GUIDE
WALKING BOOTS
BOOGIE BOARD

Activities

Imagine your family has won the lottery.

Foundation

1 Going on holiday? It's always a good idea to check out the likely weather for your holiday destination — then you know the types of clothes to take.

a Choose one location from the ten in Figure 3.20 and explain why you would like to go on holiday there.

b Give a list of what you would need to take with you for a fortnight's holiday there. Explain why you would take each item — at least five items should be linked to the climate of the area.

Target

2 You are planning a six-month trip around the world. You will need to interview members of your family who will be coming with you to find out their likes and dislikes before you plan your itinerary.

a Describe your choice of locations and what you would need to pack in your suitcase to be comfortable in each climate zone.

Extension

3 Your family are adventurous and want to travel along the Prime Meridian from London. You will need to look in an atlas to locate the Prime Meridian. Choose six countries you will stop at before returning via the International Dateline, over the North Pole to London.

a Where are you stopping?

b What is the climate like?

c What would you take in your suitcase?

◁ Figure 3.21 What to pack?

3 Weather and Climate 57

Looking at patterns

Microclimates

Earlier in this chapter (page 45), we considered how parts of your school and playground might experience different conditions. For example, some areas will be windier or hotter than others. These changes in climate, within a small area, are called **microclimates**.

Microclimates are important; for example, gardeners will choose plants for sections of their garden depending on whether the area is sunny, windy, etc. Land near water is often cooler than land further inland. Land close to trees will be less windy. Places facing south in the UK are warmer than those facing north.

Activities

1. Why is land near water cooler than land inland?

2. Draw a diagram to show why land close to trees will be less windy.

3. Why will north facing slopes in Australia be warmer than those facing south?

Rural and urban differences

There are also climatic differences between built-up (urban) areas and countryside (rural). In the cities, darker coloured surfaces and buildings absorb heat more quickly during the day. For a similar reason, we wear lighter coloured clothing in the summer to keep cooler. The amount of traffic in cities can also create heat. As a result, cities are at least 1°C warmer than rural areas in the day. At night the surfaces will release heat slowly, creating urban temperatures around 4°C higher than the surrounding rural areas.

Generally, urban areas will not be as windy as rural areas because buildings such as skyscrapers will slow the wind down. However, these tall buildings can also channel the wind and cause strong gusts.

▽ **Figure 3.22** New York street scene

Activities

Going on a temperature safari around your school:

4. Using a plan of your school, decide which areas might be the warmest and which the coldest. Give reasons for your choice.

5. Draw a route around your school grounds, which includes the warmest and the coldest sites. Mark on where you could take the temperature at regular intervals.

6. Test your answers to question 1 by following the route and recording the temperatures at each site.

Explaining patterns

A geographer will have a good idea of the climate of an area if they have the answers to the following questions:
- How far is it from the Equator? (Latitude)
- Is the area coastal or inland? (Distance from sea)
- How high is the area above sea level? (Altitude)
- From which direction do winds usually blow? (Prevailing wind)

As you read the information describing the climates of the UK and Algeria, try to remember these four questions.

Frontal rainfall

The UK is located in a position where warm air often meets cold air (a **front**). When warmer air (from the south) meets colder air (from the north) the warm air rises up over the cold air. The warm air is forced to cool as the **altitude** increases; the water vapour condenses and turns into water droplets, forming clouds. This causes rain in Britain.

Relief rainfall

The UK has areas of mountains, such as the Cambrian Mountains in North Wales and the Pennines in England. If moist air is forced upwards over the mountains, it will cool and condense, turning into water droplets, and clouds form. This causes rain in the west of Britain, before the air passes over the mountains.

Most rainfall in Britain is either **frontal** or **relief** rainfall.

Convectional rainfall

Sometimes the summers in the UK are hotter than usual. The hot sun will warm the air near the ground. The warm air will be lighter (less dense) and so it rises. As the air rises it will cool, condense and clouds will form. This can cause rain in Britain during summer.

▽ **Figure 3.23** Rainfall diagrams

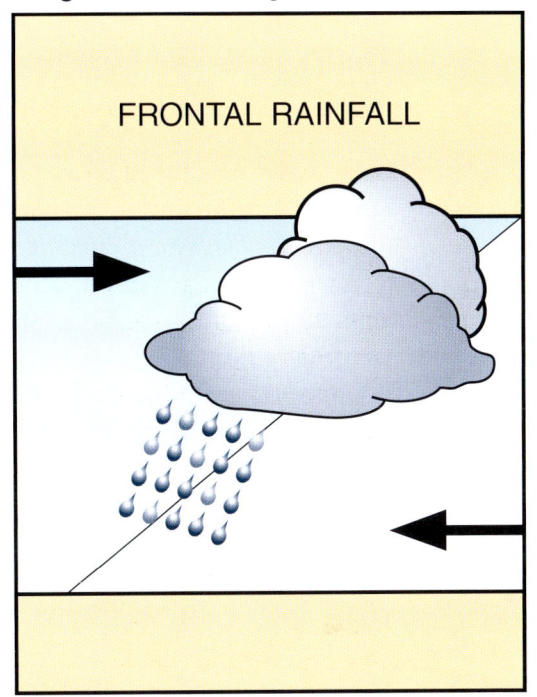

Activities

7 Copy out the diagrams in Figure 3.23 and then add the following labels to show how relief and frontal rainfall occur in Britain:
- warmer air from the south
- colder air from the north
- warm air rises up over the cold air
- warm air is forced to cool as the altitude increases
- water vapour condenses
- and turns into water droplets
- clouds form
- moist air is forced upwards over the mountains
- air cools and condenses, turning into water droplets, clouds form

3 Weather and Climate 59

Comparing the UK with Algeria

Temperate maritime climate

The UK is located to the west of the continent of Europe, between 50 and 60 degrees north of the Equator. Our location means we have a **temperate maritime climate**. As a result temperatures in Britain are never too warm nor too cold: they are mild (temperate). The temperature ranges about 15 degrees during the year. Moist winds from the sea (**maritime**) cause us to have rainfall throughout the year. Around 900 mm of rain falls on average each year.

The temperature and rainfall in the UK are influenced by the winds, which mainly blow from the west (**prevailing wind**). In summer, the prevailing westerly winds blow over the cool Atlantic Ocean. These same winds then cool down our temperatures on land and prevent hot summers. In winter, the prevailing wind blows over the relatively warmer Atlantic Ocean and the winds warm the land, preventing cold winters. Throughout the year, the winds travel over the Atlantic Ocean and pick up moisture on their way, which affects our rainfall.

Hot desert climate

The Sahara desert is found in North Africa, between 10 and 30 degrees north of the Equator. Algeria is one country found in the Sahara desert. Africa is a large **continent** and so winds lose moisture as they blow across the land. The Sahara's location means it has a hot desert climate. Temperatures are very hot in summer (up to 45°C) and stay warm in winter (12°C). There is very little rainfall; less than 250 mm a year and some months may have no rainfall at all. Night times are always very cold in the desert because there are no clouds to trap heat and so it is lost very quickly when the sun sets.

During summer time in the northern **hemisphere**, the sun will be directly overhead in the Sahara. This means that the land is heated up very quickly. Prevailing north-easterly winds blowing in the area are already warm from travelling across so much land. Even in winter, the sun is quite high in the sky, keeping the temperatures warm. However, the desert is a long way from the warming influence of any sea breezes. Any winds blowing in the area have cooled down as they travel across the land.

Warm air from the Equator will rise, cool and condense to form clouds and then fall back down to earth. The Sahara is located where the air descends. As the air falls, it will warm up and any water vapour will be **evaporated**, leaving cloudless skies and little rain. The wind does not provide any moisture because it has blown across the continent. When **convectional rain** does fall in the desert it is very heavy; the heavy rainfall on sun-baked ground often causes floods. The rainfall in desert areas is very unpredictable and the floods can occur very quickly, so they are called **flash floods**.

60 INVESTIGATING GEOGRAPHY A

Figure 3.24 Climate graph for Birmingham (altitude 163m)

Figure 3.25 Climate graph for Sahara Desert, Ain Salah, Algeria (altitude 293m)

Activities

1 Using all the information about the climates of Birmingham and Ain Salah, copy and complete the table below, Figure 3.26.

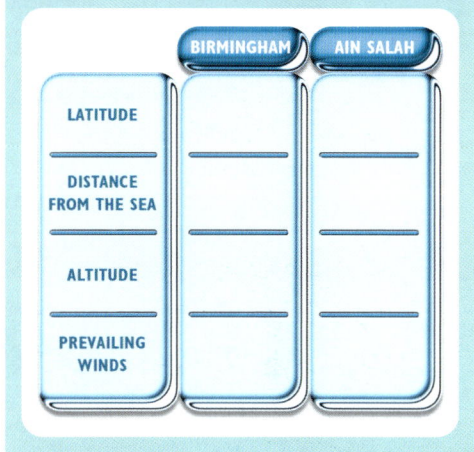

	BIRMINGHAM	AIN SALAH
LATITUDE		
DISTANCE FROM THE SEA		
ALTITUDE		
PREVAILING WINDS		

Figure 3.26 Comparisons table

2 Compare the two climate graphs for Birmingham and Ain Salah. Describe the similarities and differences, useful phrases to include are:

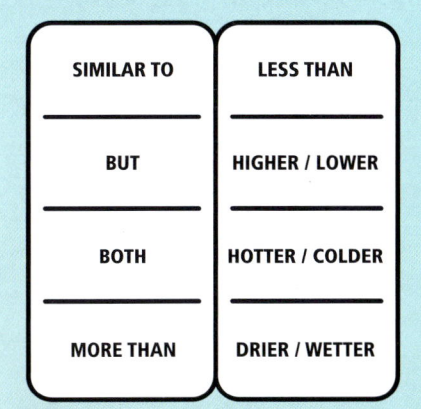

SIMILAR TO	LESS THAN
BUT	HIGHER / LOWER
BOTH	HOTTER / COLDER
MORE THAN	DRIER / WETTER

3 Give reasons for the differences in climate between Birmingham and Ain Salah. It may be useful to use the questions at the beginning of this section (page 59).

3 Weather and Climate 61

Assessment task

Background

You have been asked to help with the design of a new **biome** for the Eden Centre in Cornwall. Choose either the hot desert biome or one for the UK climate. Your teacher will tell you whether to use Design Brief A or Design Brief B.

Target task - Design Brief A

Work through the following stages to create a plan of your biome:

1 Collect information.
You need to find out about the climate (hot desert or UK) – an atlas may be useful. Find out about the plants that live in hot deserts or the UK – gardening books and garden centres will be useful for UK plants. Geography textbooks and the Internet will be useful for desert plants e.g. www.desertusa.com. Think about the colours you would use inside the biome for signs, e.g. for deserts you may choose to use reds and oranges.

2 Welcome and educate all visitors.
The biome needs to be a safe environment for visitors. You need to plan your biome for disabled visitors, children and adults. Decide how your visitors will learn about the plants and climate in hot deserts or the UK. Will you have information boards, cassette tape walks, Tour guides, etc.?

3 Draw your biome.
Draw a map of the inside of your biome. Put on plant areas, paths, information boards, entrance, exit, etc. Design a key or label the ideas.

Extension task - Design Brief B

Your presentation should be in a Design & Technology format:

1 Research.
Use a variety of resources, e.g. the Internet, landscape-architecture books, gardening books. Find out the climate for your chosen biome and the types of plants that are adapted to that climate. Collect pictures, sample colour schemes and suggestions of materials to be used in the display.

2 Analyse your research.
Consider any limitations on your research ideas, such as cost, health and safety, disabled access, vandalism, potential age of visitors.

3 Specification.
State the purpose of your design. Consider what is possible and practical. Visitors should have the opportunity to learn about the climate, the plants and plant adaptations (how plants survive).

4 Ideas.
Once you are clear what has to be done, select possible ideas and sketches from your initial research that may be suitable.

5 Ideas development.
Make a decision on your final design, and produce a plan of the biome showing where plants, information boards, pathways will be situated.

Review

Did you know?

The coldest, inhabited place in the world is Norilsk, in Russia, where the average temperaure for the year is −10.9°C. The coldest recorded temperature ever was −89.2°C in Antarctica in 1983.

The highest amount of rainfall within 24 hours was 1 870 mm, recorded in La Reunion Island, Indian Ocean in 1952. The highest amount of rainfall recorded in 12 months was 26 461 mm in Assam in 1860. The wettest place is Mawsynran, in India which receives 11 873 mm per year on average.
The highest amount of rainfall within a minute was 31.2 mm, recorded in the USA in 1956.

The fastest wind speed recorded on Earth is 231 mph (371 kmph), recorded in New Hampshire, USA, in 1934.
The fastest wind speed recorded in the UK 144 mph (231 kmph), recorded in Scotland in 1967.

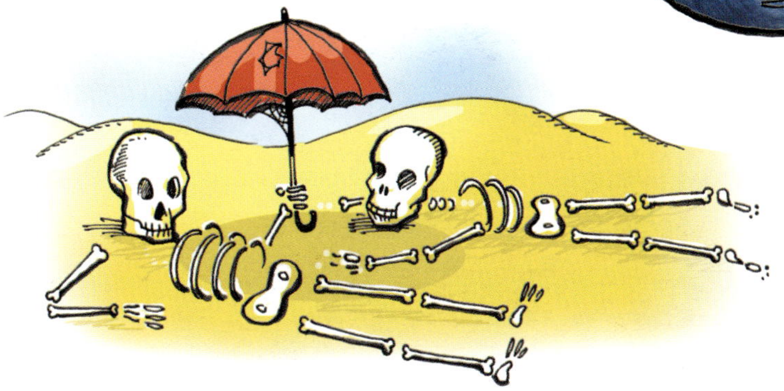

The hottest, inhabited place in the world is Djibouti, in Djibouti, where the average temperature is 30°C. The hottest recorded temperature ever was 57.7°C at Al' Aziziyah in Libya in 1922. The highest temperature ever recorded in the UK was 37.1°C.

In the Atacama desert, Chile, no rain was recorded in the 400 years before 1971. The longest drought in the UK was in 1893, when London did not receive any rain for 73 days.

△ **Figure 3.27** Weather facts

Activities

1. Which of these records do you think is the most amazing? Why?

2. Look back through all of the work you have done for this unit. Write down the three most interesting things you have learnt.

3 Weather and Climate 63

4 Economic Activity

How does hair provide a living?

Before...

△ **Figure 4.1**

Rasu and his family are pilgrims. They have travelled to the temple at Sri Venkatasvara to sell their hair as an offering to the Hindu god Vishnu. Along the road the barbers who work in the fields next to the road pounce and shave a strip of hair from each pilgrim to claim their scalp after they have visited the temple. Rasu and his family will then receive money for selling their hair.

64 INVESTIGATING GEOGRAPHY A

After.....

△ Figure 4.2

Hair from barber shops, temples and from villages is bought. Children work unprotected in poor conditions to sort the hair. They work an eight-hour day for 25p. The best quality hair is exported to western wig makers for £20 a kilo. The rest is chopped and sold to chemical companies who make amino acids for use in food and medicine manufacture. A full head of hair is worth £6, a significant sum to a poor village woman.

Activities

1 Tell the person sitting next to you your first impressions of these two images. Could you imagine yourself selling your hair?

2 What questions would you like to ask the people in the photographs to find out more about their lives?

4 Economic Activity

The World of Work

Different jobs

There are different jobs in many types of industry. These can be put into different categories.
- **Primary industry** is involved with the extracting of raw materials from the land or sea.
- **Secondary industry** processes the raw materials into a manufactured product for a consumer or as a component for another manufacturer.
- **Tertiary industry** provides a service either for an individual customer or a company.
- **Quaternary industry** deals with information and information technology.

You can decide in which category a job is by asking three questions. First, are they taking anything from the natural world? Yes, means a primary job. No, means asking a second question: are they making something? Yes, means a secondary job. No, means a tertiary or quaternary occupation. Lastly, are they helping people directly? Yes would suggest a tertiary job. No may mean quaternary.

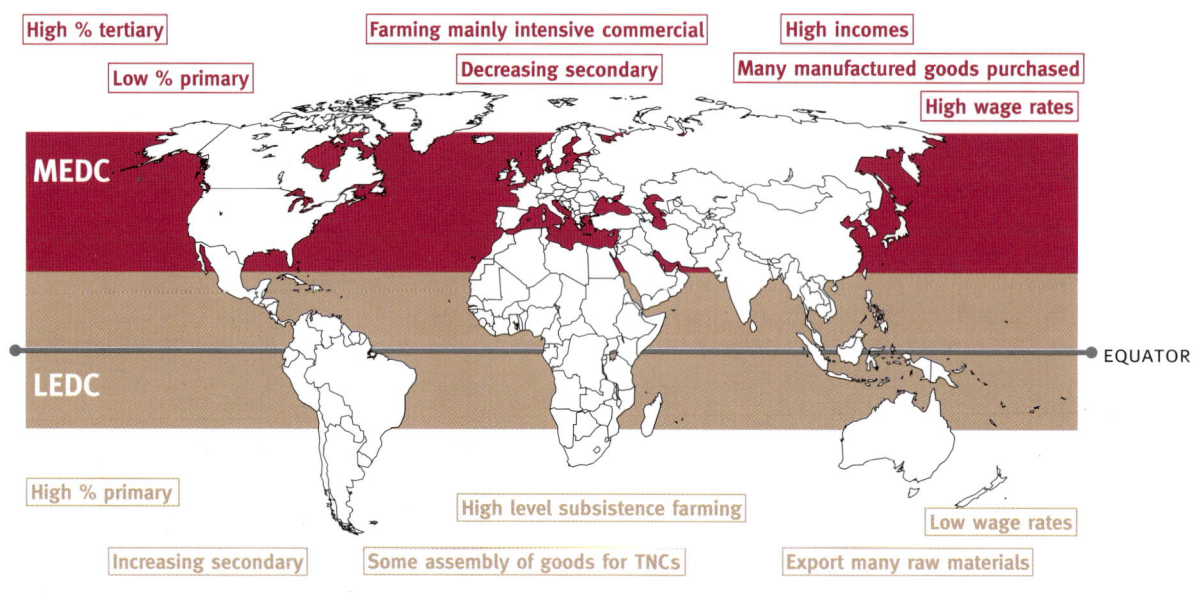

△ **Figure 4.3** Comparing countries

MEDC: High % tertiary; Low % primary; Farming mainly intensive commercial; Decreasing secondary; High incomes; Many manufactured goods purchased; High wage rates

LEDC: High % primary; Increasing secondary; High level subsistence farming; Some assembly of goods for TNCs; Low wage rates; Export many raw materials

Comparing countries

In **LEDCs** the type and number of jobs is different to **MEDCs** like the UK (see Figure 4.3). The richer and more developed a country is, the lower the proportion of people who work in the primary and secondary sectors. In most MEDCs the largest employer is the tertiary sector. These countries can collect enough taxes to pay for public services like health and education. Also many people spend money on leisure activities and consumer goods. This demand creates more tertiary jobs.

Many LEDCs depend on their raw materials and agriculture to provide work. These countries have lacked the investment to develop jobs in manufacturing. Instead people desperate to earn a living have created jobs in the tertiary sector. These form part of the **informal economy** which meets many local needs. These jobs do not pay taxes which a government could use to improve job opportunities and social services for the population.

What does it mean for me?

EACH DAY I WORK... I EARN...

I HAVE...

I LIVE IN...

MY NAME IS...

who?
what?
where?
why?

I LIVE IN...

EACH DAY I...

I HAVE...

△ **Figure 4.4** Child labourer

▷ **Figure 4.5** Children in Britain

Activities

1 Study Figure 4.3.

a Write three sentences to show how the North and the South employment structures are different.

b Suggest why there are more primary jobs in LEDCs.

c Write a list of ten jobs you would expect a 12-year-old to do in the UK and in an LEDC. Suggest reasons for the differences.

d Do you think it is right that so many children in the LEDCs have to work? Explain three reasons to support your point of view.

2 Study Figures 4.4 and 4.5.

a Plan an interview about how each will earn their living in the future.

b Suggest why there is likely to be a difference between the answers.

4 Economic Activity

How and why is the United Kingdom employment structure changing?

The percentages of people doing the different types of jobs vary from region to region. The jobs in an area can tell us about its industrial history and geography, for example, raw materials and places that have specialised industry.

REGION	PRIMARY%	SECONDARY%	TERTIARY%
1 South East	2	14	84
2 London	Less than 1	8	92
3 Eastern	2	18	80
4 South West	2	17	81
5 East Midlands	3	26	71
6 West Midlands	1	27	72
7 North West	1	21	78
8 Yorkshire/Humbershire	2	22	76
9 North	1	23	76
10 Wales	2	22	76
11 Scotland	3	16	81
12 Northern Ireland	4	18	78

△ **Figure 4.6** Regional employment structure, 1999

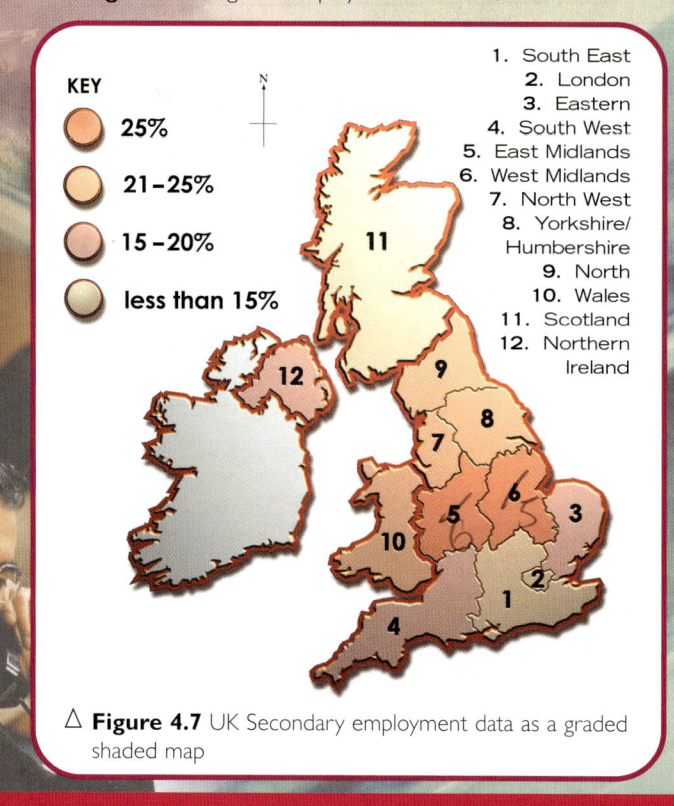

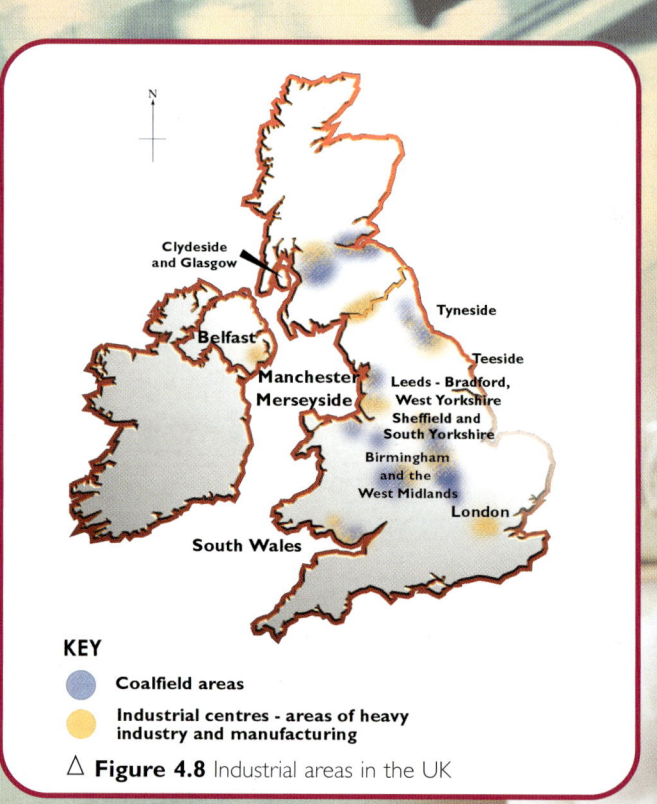

KEY
- 25%
- 21–25%
- 15–20%
- less than 15%

1. South East
2. London
3. Eastern
4. South West
5. East Midlands
6. West Midlands
7. North West
8. Yorkshire/Humbershire
9. North
10. Wales
11. Scotland
12. Northern Ireland

△ **Figure 4.7** UK Secondary employment data as a graded shaded map

KEY
- Coalfield areas
- Industrial centres - areas of heavy industry and manufacturing

Clydeside and Glasgow, Tyneside, Belfast, Teeside, Manchester Merseyside, Leeds - Bradford, West Yorkshire Sheffield and South Yorkshire, Birmingham and the West Midlands, South Wales, London

△ **Figure 4.8** Industrial areas in the UK

68 INVESTIGATING GEOGRAPHY A

Some reasons for the changes

In recent years, many coalfield areas and heavy industrial regions have lost their traditional jobs for a number of reasons:

- foreign competition
- raw materials running out, for example, coal and iron ore deposits becoming exhausted
- new materials and technologies replacing traditional products, for example, plastics or natural gas
- robot technology replacing workers, for example, in car manufacturing
- cheaper labour costs abroad makes their products less expensive
- lack of investment in technology and new factories, and lack of government help.

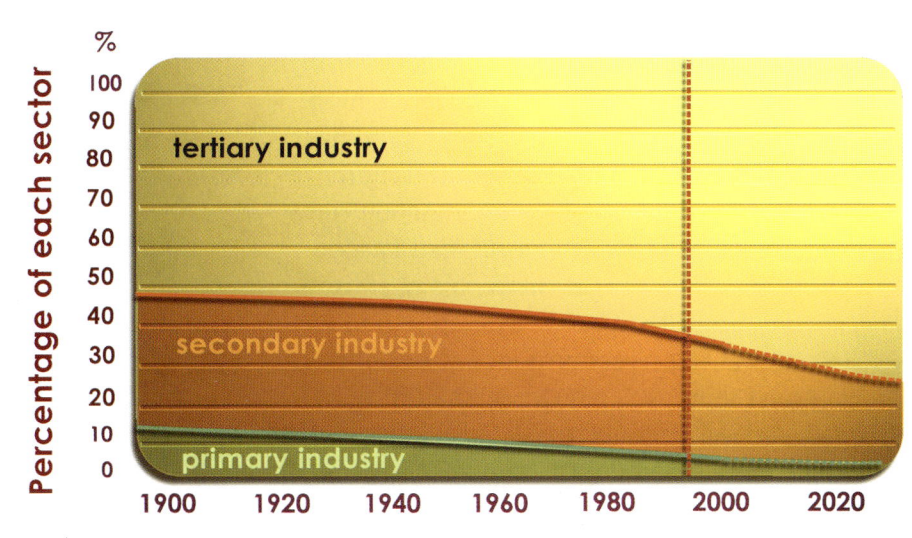

△ **Figure 4.9** Changes in the United Kingdom employment structure

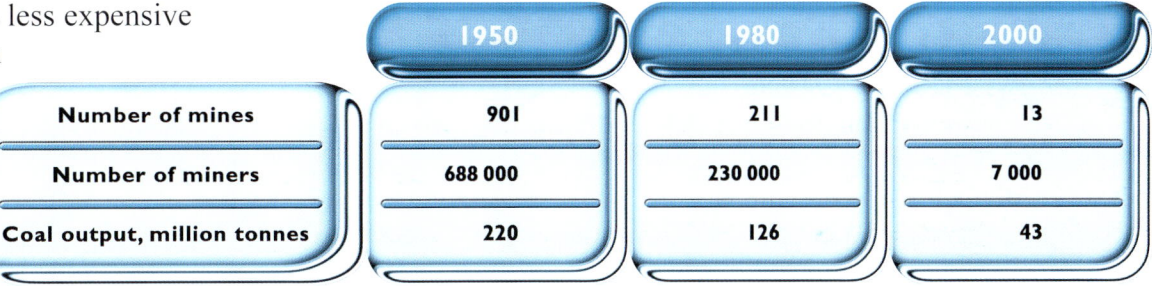

	1950	1980	2000
Number of mines	901	211	13
Number of miners	688 000	230 000	7 000
Coal output, million tonnes	220	126	43

△ **Figure 4.10** Changes in coal mining

Activities

Foundation

1 Look at Figure 4.6. Which are the top three regions for primary industry in the UK? Label these onto a map.

2 Look at Figure 4.6. Which are the top four regions for tertiary industry in the UK? Label these onto a map.

Target

3 Use Figure 4.7 with Figure 4.8 to describe the distribution of secondary industry. Suggest reasons for this distribution.

4 Use Figure 4.9 to describe how primary, secondary and tertiary industry have changed since 1900. Why have these changes happened?

Extension

5 Draw a concept map or flow diagram to show why the coalfield regions have lost so many jobs.

6 Suggest the problems caused by this for the people and the region?

4 Economic Activity 69

What has happened to Sheffield Steel?

World trends

In recent years there has been a world wide increase in total steel production. However, whilst world production has increased, there have been different trends in the steel-producing countries. Sheffield has a long steel history. The region had the raw materials coal, iron ore and limestone easily available to make steel. The rivers provided water power and there was a huge demand in the UK and the colonies for the specialist steel products like tools or knives. Steel has since declined in Sheffield. The steel it produces is expensive and the local raw materials exhausted. The area has only tradition and a skilled workforce left.

Today, the UK imports steel from LEDCs. In 1948 the top steel producer nations were the USA, UK and other European countries. By 1995 the top steel producer nations were Japan, China, the USA, South Korea and Brazil. These countries have modern steelworks, plentiful raw materials and a cheap labour force.

	1948	1970	1980	1990	1995
World	155	593	690	723	720

△ **Figure 4.11** World steel production (million tonnes)

	1948	1970	1980	1990	1995
MEDC Germany	6	5	52	37	37
Japan	2	93	111	98	98
UK	15	28	11	16	16
USA	80	119	101	83	87
LEDC China	1	18	37	80	88
India	2	7	9	18	19
S. Korea	0	1	6	28	34

△ **Figure 4.12** Selected steel production

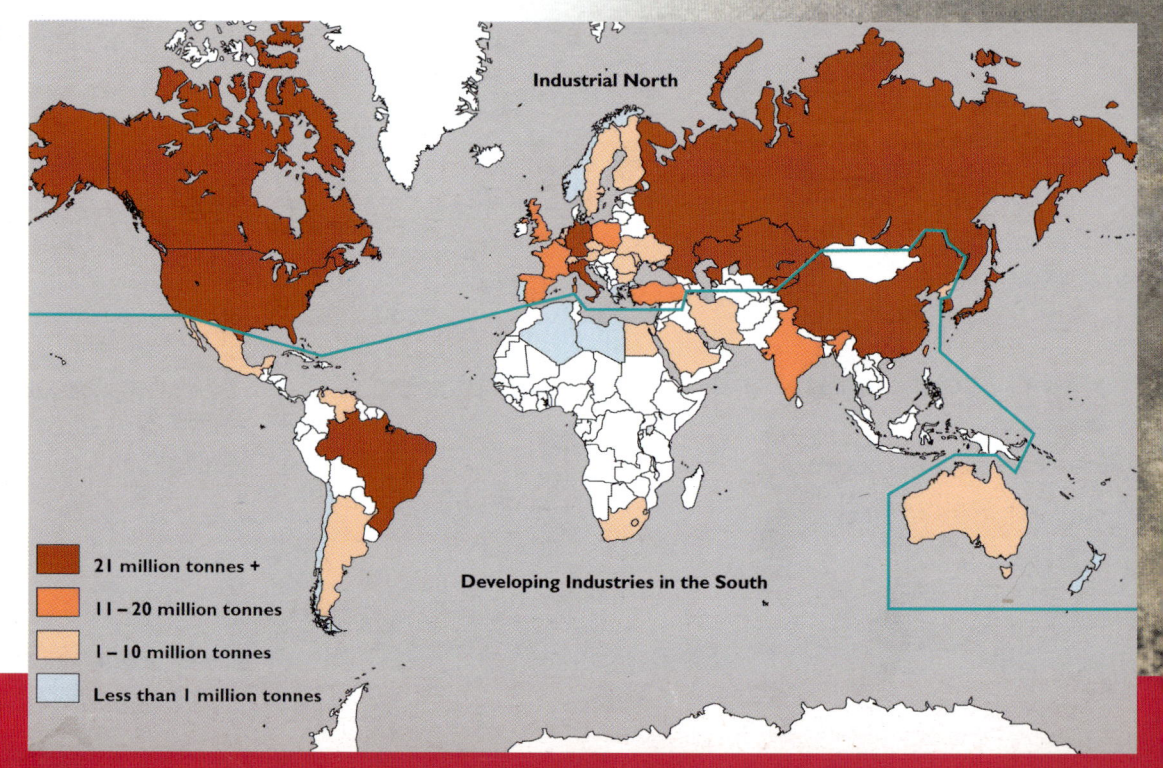

▷ **Figure 4.13** World steel producers

- 21 million tonnes +
- 11–20 million tonnes
- 1–10 million tonnes
- Less than 1 million tonnes

Industrial North

Developing Industries in the South

Activities

Working as a pair, complete the tasks below and present your graphs and summaries as a poster describing the changes in world steel production.

1 World trend

a On a piece of graph paper, plot a line graph to show world steel production.

b Use your graph and the table to complete this description:

> 'The world production of steel has ..... since 1948. In 1948 ..... million tonnes was produced. In 1995 this had increased to ..... million tonnes. This is an increase of ..... in this time.'

2 Steel production in MEDCs

a Study Figure 4.12. Is steel production increasing or decreasing in MEDCs?

b Draw a bar chart to show the steel production for the UK and then one for Japan.

c Describe the trend for these MEDCs.

d Does Japan show a similar trend to the UK and Germany?

3 Steel production in LEDCs

a Study Figure 4.12. Is steel production in the LEDCs increasing or decreasing?

b Draw a bar chart to show the steel production in South Korea.

c Which two countries have increased their production the most?

4 Summary: Comparing LEDCs with MEDCs

a Compare the steel production trend in the MEDCs and LEDCs. Use Figure 4.13 to locate the main steel producing countries. You can use these sentence prompts to help:

World steel production is .....

The trend for steel production in the MEDCs is .....

For example in the UK steel production in 1948 was .....

This trend is found in other MEDCs such as .....

However, in LEDCs the trend for steel production is .....

For example in China steel production in 1948 was .....

This trend is found in other LEDCs such as .....

One reason for the decline in steel in the UK is .....

Another reason is .....

However, the LEDCs are able to increase steel production because .....

LEDCs sell steel to MEDCs because .....

In the future steel production in MEDCs will .....

But in the LEDCs steel production will continue to .....

4 Economic Activity 71

What happened to the Lower Don valley?

The lower Don Valley was the centre of Sheffield Steel production. Old photographs show hundreds of men eating their lunch sat alongside the Attercliffe Road. The noise of the steelworks could be heard for miles whilst furnace lights glowed in the night skies. Today the steelworks have closed. One or two large producers remain along with a few specialist works. Since 1960 over 18 000 steel jobs have been lost. For every steel job, another three services and supplier jobs were lost. The people became unemployed and the Lower Don Valley derelict. There were no other industries in the area. The Lower Don Valley went into economic decline.

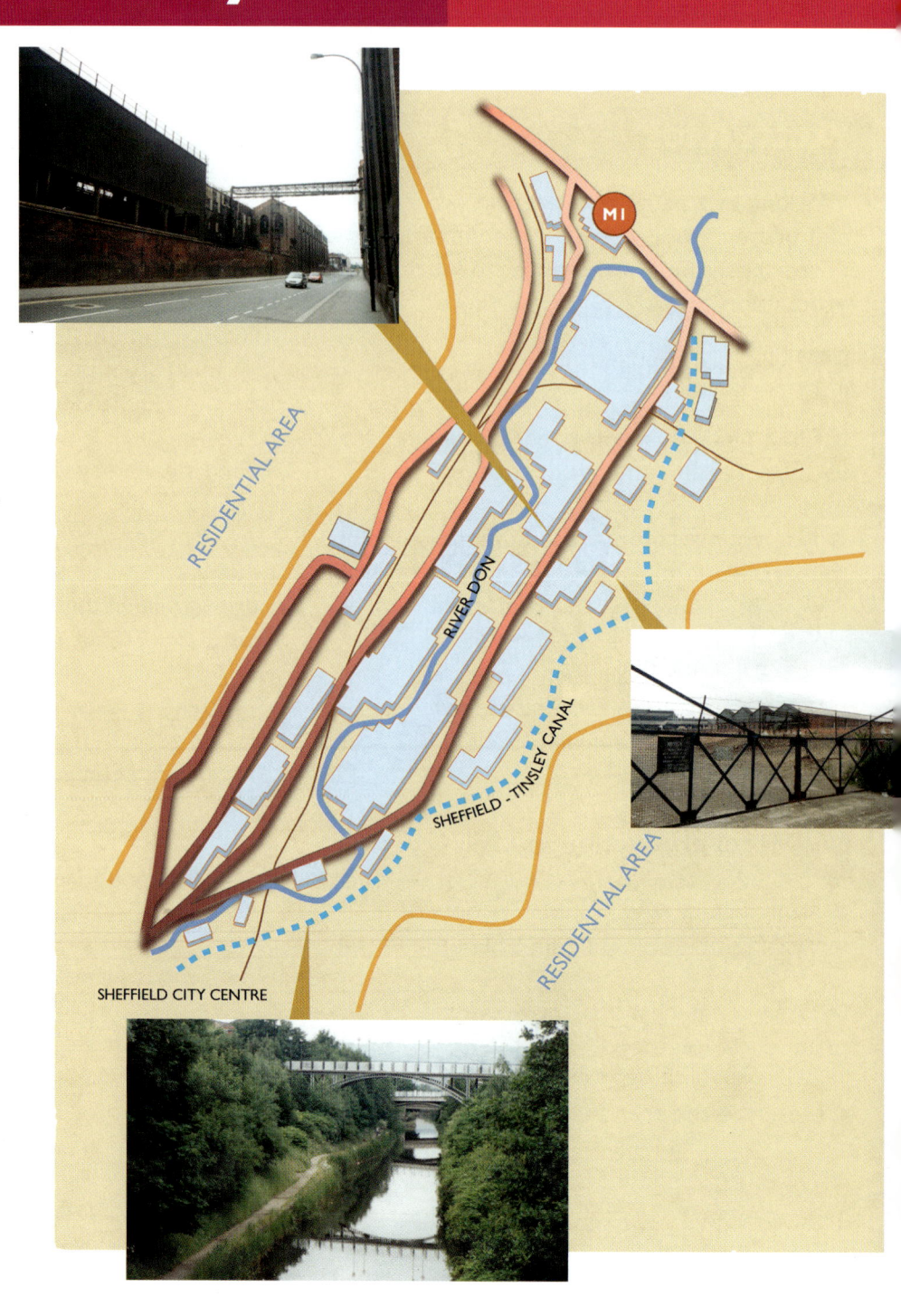

▷ **Figure 4.14** Sketch map locating the Lower Don Valley

❯ Regeneration

Since 1990 the Lower Don has been regenerated. The Sheffield Development Corporation (SDC) was set up by government to work with the City Council. The plan was to reclaim and redevelop the Lower Don Valley.

SDC has:
- helped create at least 18 000 new jobs
- attracted many new service industries into the area
- improved transport links through the area
- cleared and improved many areas of **derelict** land.

72 INVESTIGATING GEOGRAPHY A

However, local people do not feel they have all benefited from the developments. Many live outside but work in the development zone whilst others lack the skills to be employed. New companies often bring existing workers with them. Others complain that the wages were lower than before and the new jobs are low paid, low skilled and favour part-time, especially women, workers.

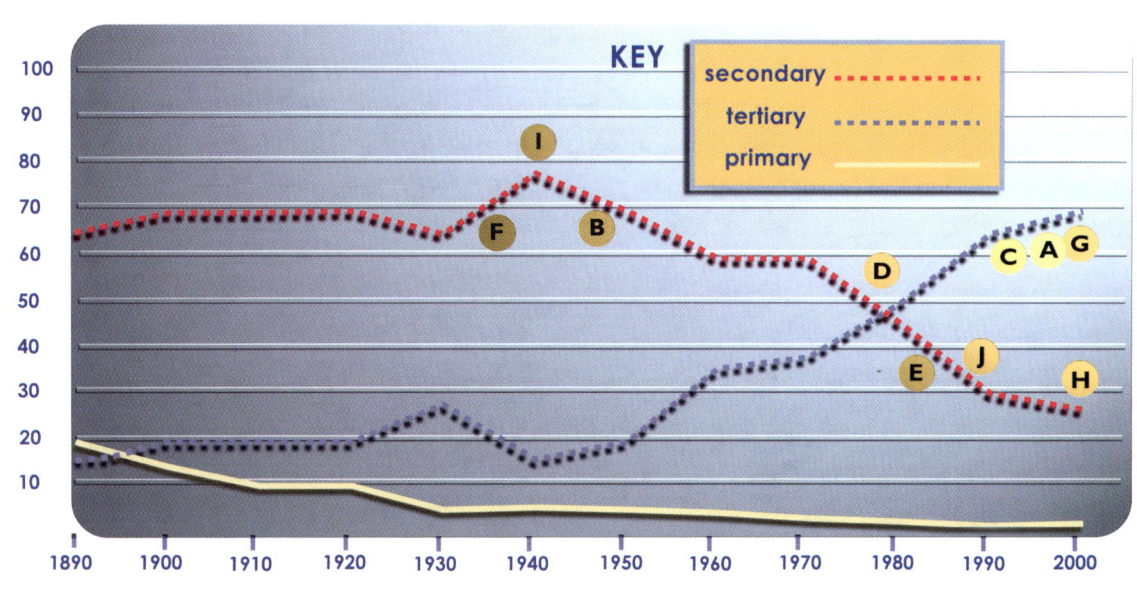

△ **Figure 4.15** Changes in the employment structure of Sheffield

Activities

1 Study the statements below carefully and decide which one you think matches best with the points marked by letters on Figure 4.15.

1 Jim gets a job as a security guard at the new shopping mall.	2 Jim loses his job at the steelworks after 30 years.	3 Marjorie takes her grandson to see 'Disney on Ice' at the Arena.	4 Paul gets a job at Abbey National's call centre in the Don Valley.	5 River Don is yellow with pollution.
6 World War Two means high demand for Sheffield steel.	7 China's steel production overtakes the UK.	8 Don Valley used as location for nuclear war films.	9 Many school leavers taken on as apprentices by steel firms.	10 Kingfishers seen living by River Don.

2 Draw an outline sketch of one of the photos in Figure 4.14. Label it with as many different adjectives to describe the features shown.

3 Imagine you live in the area shown by the photos in Figure 4.14. Write a letter to your local councillor describing the situation and making suggestions for how it should be improved.

4 Economic Activity 73

Where does industry locate and why?

Industry will choose the site which offers the best and cheapest **access** to its suppliers and market. A good **location** can help reduce costs. Industries have different location needs. A coal mine is best located on a coalfield; an engineer needs to be near other engineers; and a distribution company needs access to good road links. Figure 4.16 summarises these factors.

△ **Figure 4.16** Location factors

While many factors are logical choices, the attitudes and values of the decision-makers can be based on what the area looks like or where the owner wants to live.

Some industries continue in a location which has since lost its main reason for being there. Sheffield steel continues because of its skilled workforce and industrial links despite its raw materials being imported. This is called **industrial inertia**.

Industries must to be able to supply or meet the needs of their customers. A league football club can be a large employer. Can you suggest jobs which are associated with a football league club?

Chesterfield Football Club was established in 1874. It established a football ground at Saltergate. This is close to the town centre and surrounded by Victorian housing. People used to walk to the home games. The Saltergate ground urgently needs to be developed to meet the FA's specifications. It once held 32 000, but it is limited today to 7 000. The choice is either to redevelop Saltergate or move to a purpose-built ground.

Where should Chesterfield FC be?

Figure 4.17 shows some possible locations. On match days Saltergate is **congested,** with parking being difficult. The local residents complain of the disruption and blocked roads.

The new site needs car parking space; access to public transport, and must be away from residential areas.

▽ Figure 4.17 Saltergate

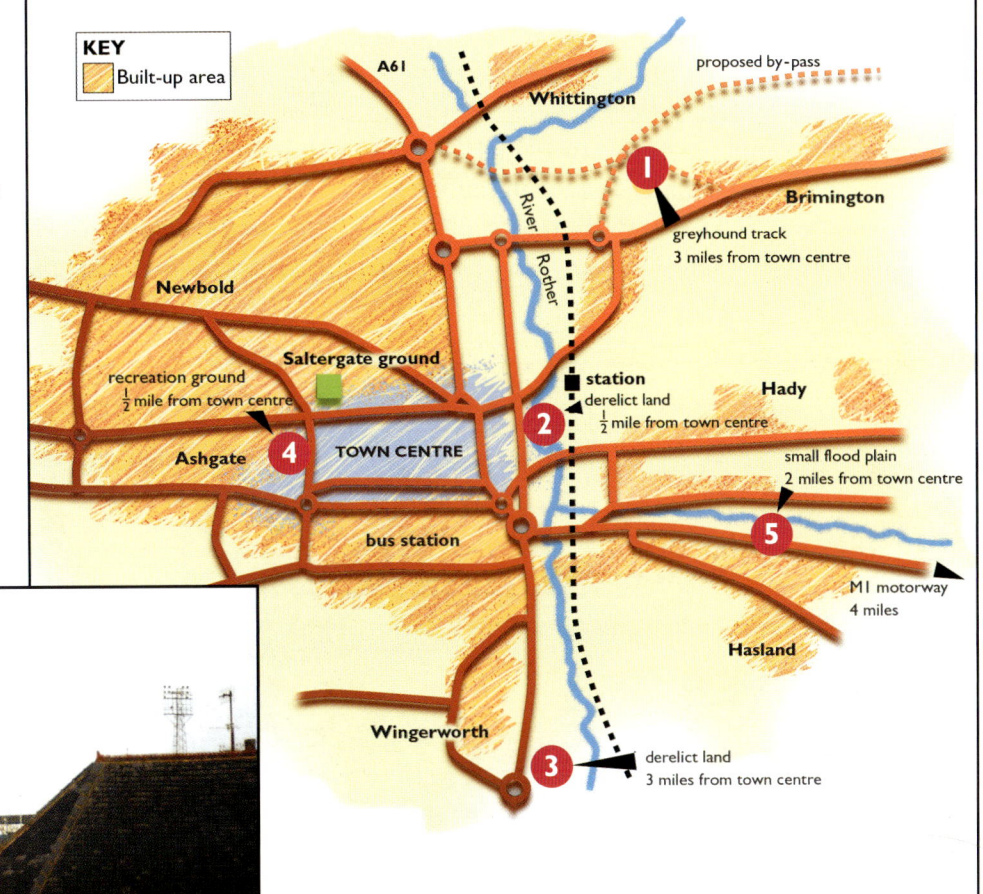

△ Figure 4.18 Some possible locations for Chesterfield FC

Activities

Foundation

1. Describe the problems of the present site as shown in Figure 4.17.

2. Give one advantage and one disadvantage for each of the possible sites shown on Figure 4.18.

3. Which site do you think is the best and why?

Target

4. Which of the possible sites in Figure 4.18 do you think would be the best location for a new ground for Chesterfield FC? Present your choice as an annotated map.

Extension

5. Suggest and justify five locational requirements that are important for a new football ground.

6. To what extent does each of the possible sites in Figure 4.18 meet your locational requirements?

4 Economic Activity 75

Who makes the clothes you wear?

Each year £23 billion is spent on clothes in Britain, over half of which were made overseas. Most come from Asia where the garment industry has grown rapidly since the 1980s. However, the number of jobs in British clothes factories has fallen steeply in recent years. In 1980 there were over one million jobs, by 2000 this had fallen to 200 000.

Cheaper imports have encouraged companies to relocate to countries which have lower wages and production costs. In real terms the price of making clothes has become cheaper. Major chain stores which sell fashion and brand name companies have insisted on low production costs from their suppliers to remain competitive.

◁ **Figure 4.19** A jeans factory in Ras Jebel, Tunisia. The trained machinists earn 58p an hour.

This work provides much needed income. But many have to work long hours, in poor conditions for very low wages, 35p a day in Indonesia and 63p a day in Bangladesh (see Figure 4.20). In those countries with better conditions there is pressure to reduce costs or lose the overseas clothes contracts.

Textiles production relies on many other components. In West Africa, cotton is grown to supply companies. Farmers use chemicals to promote growth and control pests but this also damages their health. Cotton is labour intensive and pickers earn 50p a day. The farmers make £10 profit per ton of cotton. Continued crops of cotton reduce the soil fertility and yields fall.

Other textile components rely on LEDCs. The brass zips or jean rivets manufactured in Japan are made from zinc and copper ore imported from South African mines. Here concern about how pollution affects local mining communities is balanced against the benefits of the mine to the local economy.

Clothing is a global industry. There are worldwide links between producers and consumers. Large companies are looking for the cheapest and best source of clothes. Clothes labels often identify where they are made but do not describe the conditions where the person made the item. As we demand cheaper clothes and fashion, there is a pressure to keep wages low and working conditions poor.

Country	Population	Wages £ per hour in textiles	Annual income per person $
China	1 185 000 000	0.35	620
Bangladesh	118 342 000	0.38	240
Indonesia	198 644 000	0.30	980
USA	263 563 000	6.80	27 000
UK	58 306 000	6.50	18 700

△ **Figure 4.20** Comparing incomes in textile producing countries

△ **Figure 4.21** Replica football shirts

Activities

1 a Find the country of origin for five items of your clothing.

b Produce a summary table for each item of clothing and country. You could use a spreadsheet to handle this data.

c Present this information on a world outline as a dot map.

d Describe your finished map.

e List five general points that you can make about the origins of clothing in the 21st century.

f Compare your findings with another class in your school, which has completed this survey.

2 a With a partner brainstorm at least ten jobs in the making of a replica shirt.

b Sort these jobs into groups; you decide which groups.

c Explain how you decided on your groups.

3 Study Figure 4.20.

a Use the jobs you identified in question 2. Arrange in order of wages from lowest to highest, how much you think each job would be paid.

b Which jobs do you think would be found in an LEDC and in an MEDC?

c Explain your answer.

4 Economic Activity 77

What are transnational companies: are they good or bad?

Sportswear: a case study

Sportswear is big business. Some companies make up to 90 million pairs of sports shoes a year. These companies can spend up to one billion dollars on marketing and the promotion of their products. This included sponsorship of national football teams, tennis players, golfers and basketball stars.

Many of these companies have moved production from America and Europe to South Korea and Taiwan. Other countries such as Indonesia, Bangladesh and China also produce sportswear goods for these firms. These regions offer a cheap and flexible workforce. Indonesia is one of the biggest production centres making 7 million pairs of shoes a month and employing 90 000 workers for one company alone. The minimum legal wage is $2.46 per day, but this is making Indonesia uncompetitive and firms are looking to expand production in China and former European communist states like Romania, where costs are lower.

It has also been estimated that a worker sewing a ski jacket earned 51p per jacket. The same jacket sells for £100 in the UK.

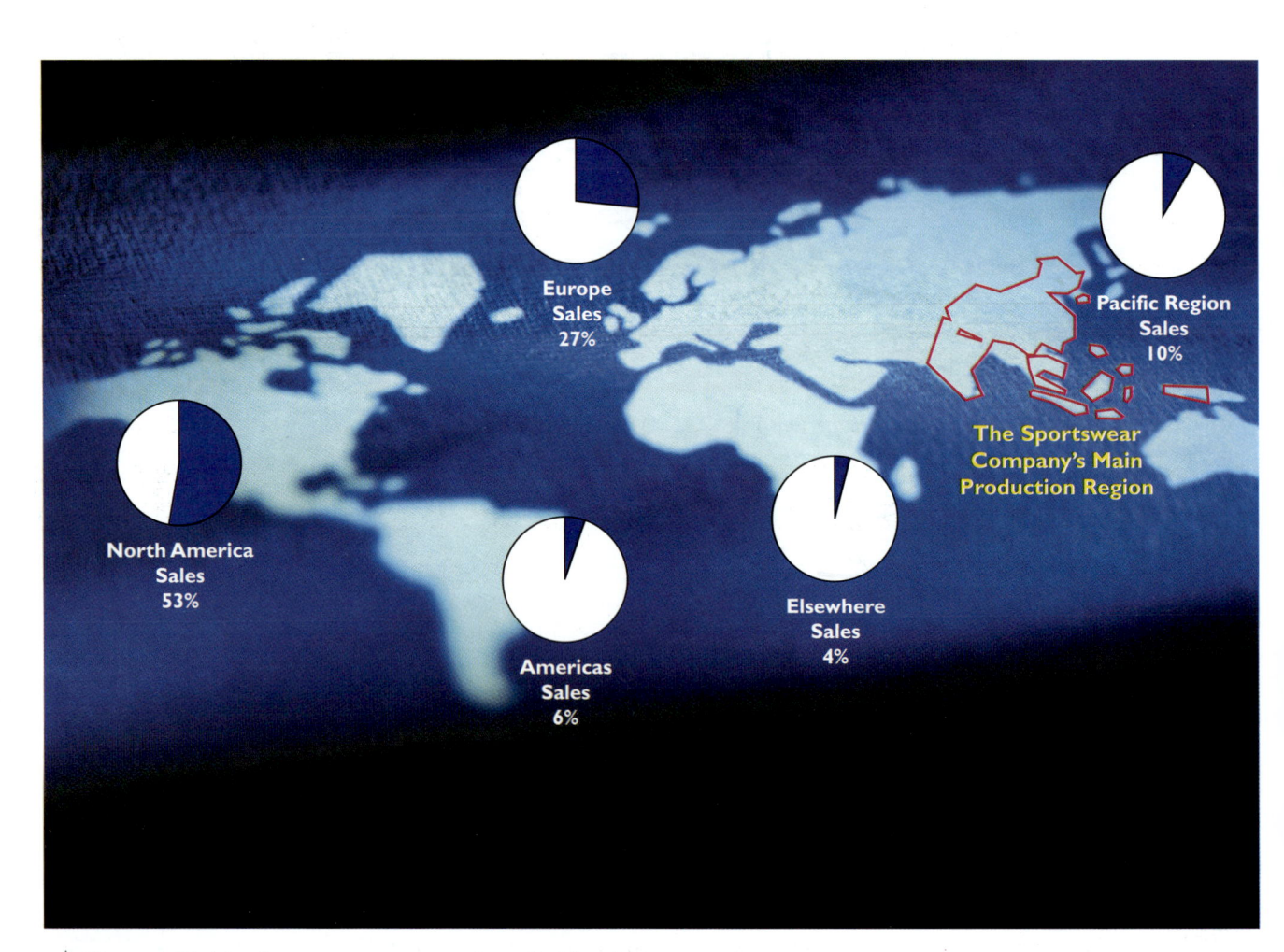

△ **Figure 4.22** A leading sportswear company's worldwide sales

Transnational companies

(TNCs) operate on a worldwide scale. Figure 4.23 shows where a major jeans company source their materials for a pair of £20 jeans.

Many transnational companies have incomes bigger than the countries they trade with. This means they are very powerful economic forces! So why do many LEDCs encourage TNCs to locate in their countries? What are the benefits for the LEDC?

Figure 4.23 Origin of the components for a major jeans company

Labels on map:
- N. Ireland (thread)
- Germany (dyes - for jeans)
- France (polyester rope)
- Italy (denim made)
- Turkey (pumice stone - for stone washing)
- Japan (zips & rivets)
- Spain (dyed thread)
- Algeria (garment assembly)
- Pakistan (cotton - for lining and pockets)
- West Africa (cotton - for denim)
- Namibia (copper)
- Australia (zinc)

Figure 4.24 Advantages and disadvantages of TNCs to LEDCs

PROVIDES JOBS	PROVIDES NEW FACTORIES	PAYS LOW WAGES	ENCOURAGES POOR WORKING CONDITIONS	INCREASES EXPORTS
ATTRACTS OTHER TNCs TO SET UP	USES LATEST TECHNOLOGY	PROVIDES EXPERT MANAGERS	INCREASES COUNTRY'S SKILLED WORKFORCE	INFLUENCES GOVERNMENT DECISIONS
SLOWS DOWN LEDCs DEVELOPING OWN INDUSTRIES	CAN CAUSE ENVIRONMENTAL DAMAGE AND POLLUTION	INCREASES COUNTRY'S WEALTH	MAY PROVIDE BENEFITS FOR WORKERS LIKE HEALTHCARE	HELPS IMPROVE ROADS AND POWER SUPPLIES

Activities

Foundation

1 What is a transnational company (TNC)?

2 Give two examples of TNCs.

3 Give one advantage and one disadvantage of TNCs to LEDCs.

Target

4 Study Figure 4.22. What do you notice about the company's sales and production?

5 Study Figure 4.24. Choose nine statements which explain why an LEDC would want to attract a transnational company. For each statement say why you choose it.

Extension

6 Do you think that LEDCs should encourage TNCs to set up in their country? Give reasons for your opinion.

4 Economic Activity 79

Assessment tasks

Background

The Lower Don Valley in Sheffield was devastated by the collapse of the steel industry, and the engineering that relied on steel, in the 1980s. However, several developments have helped to regenerate the area. The largest has been the Meadowhall Shopping Centre. Other possible developments include:

A small airport
This will need to be close to both Rotherham and Sheffield and have a runway at least one km long.

A technology park
This will need space to build small laboratory-style units with access to the city centre and the two universities there.

A retail park
This will need a large flat area to build store units and space for car parking. Easy access to the motorway would be good for business.

A group of small workshops
This will need to be inside the Sheffield Development Corporation (SDC) boundary to attract the grants that are available.

An athletics stadium
This will need main road access as well as public transport close by. It will also need space for a 400 m running track and all the stands and other facilities.

An international arena
This will need main road access and if close to the stadium they could share parking space. This will also need good public transport.

△ **Figure 4.25** An aerial view of the Lower Don Valley

△ **Figure 4.26** OS map Lower Don Valley ├──┼──┼──┼──┤ tramline

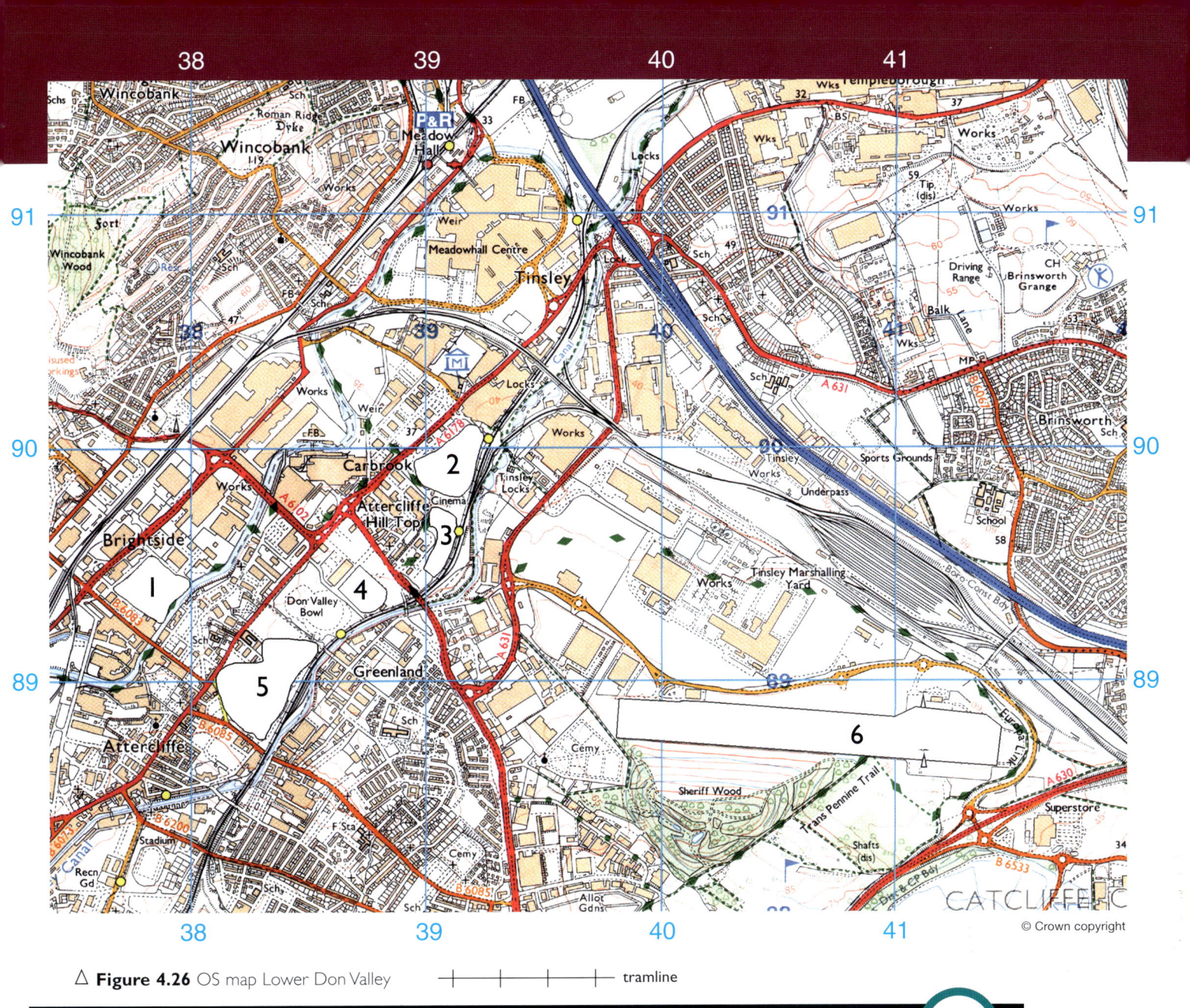

Target tasks

1 Draw an outline map of Figure 4.26. Mark on the following features: main roads, canal, River Don, railway, the M1, Meadowhall Shopping Centre, the location of possible sites for the proposed developments. Add a key to your map.

2 For each of the proposed developments, choose the best location. Label these on your map.

3 Give at least one reason for each of your decisions. You can use these sentence starts to help write your explanation:

I have decided to put the ..... at site .....

The reason for my decision is .....

This development also needs ..... so that .....

The next development, the ..... should be located at site .....

The reason for my decision is .....

This development also needs ..... so that .....

4 Suggest one other development which would help the redevelop-ment of the Lower Don Valley. Locate this on your map and give at least one reason for your suggestion.

4 Economic Activity 81

Assessment tasks

Extension tasks

1
a Make a copy of Figure 4.27.

b Study the location of each site.

c Complete the table by noting the main features of each site.

d Suggest the most appropriate development for each site.

Site on map	Location factors for each site						Proposed development
	Main road	Rail and tram	Flat land	Work force	Land uses	Others	
Meadowhall							Shopping centre
A							
B							
C							
D							
E							
F							
G							
H							
I							

△ **Figure 4.27** Summary table

2 Study your completed table.

a What are the common features needed to attract new industry to locate in the Lower Don Valley?

b Suggest what else could be done to make the Lower Don Valley more attractive for new industry.

c Suggest three other types of development that could be attracted to locate in the Lower Don Valley. Why might they be attracted to this area?

3 How would the people who live in the Lower Don Valley benefit from these developments?

Review

What do I think about economic activity?

△ Figure 4.28

△ Figure 4.29

△ Figure 4.30

Activities

1 Choose one of the photographs above.

a List five points about this type of economic activity.

b How might this activity change in the future? Why?

c How is this activity connected with other jobs and places?

2 Read through all the work you have done about economic activities. Write a sentence to describe:

a One thing that has surprised you.

b One thing about industry in an LEDC.

c How industry is changing in the UK.

3 Read through all of the work you have done for this unit. Write down five bullet points to summarise what you have learnt. Compile a class list on the board.

4 Economic Activity

5 National Parks

What is special about a National Park?

A **National Park** is an area that has been given special planning laws to try and make sure that it is conserved and looked after. It is an area of outstanding natural beauty.

△ Figure 5.2

△ Figure 5.1

▽ Figure 5.3

84 INVESTIGATING GEOGRAPHY A

streams
quiet
wild
traditional
countryside
pretty
peaceful
free
clean
crowded
open
villages
boring
isolated
cottages
tourists
moors
daytrips
old
green
footpaths
farmland
relaxed

△ **Figure 5.6** Responses to the photographs

△ **Figure 5.4**

▽ **Figure 5.5**

Activities

1 Read the words in Figure 5.6. Match these words with the photograph in Figures 5.1 to 5.5.

2 Think of three adjectives for each photograph that helps to describe it.

3 With a partner use the information on these pages to write a 50-word definition/description of a National Park.

4 Now discuss your definition with the class and agree a group definition of a National Park. Write this definition on a large piece of paper for display on the wall. Check it and revise the definition as you work on this topic.

5 National Parks

What do we already know about parks?

We all have an image in our minds when we hear the word 'park'. Most people who live in towns think of a children's playground in a **public park**, like Figure 5.7.

▽ **Figure 5.7** A public park

▽ **Figure 5.8** Concept map for a public park

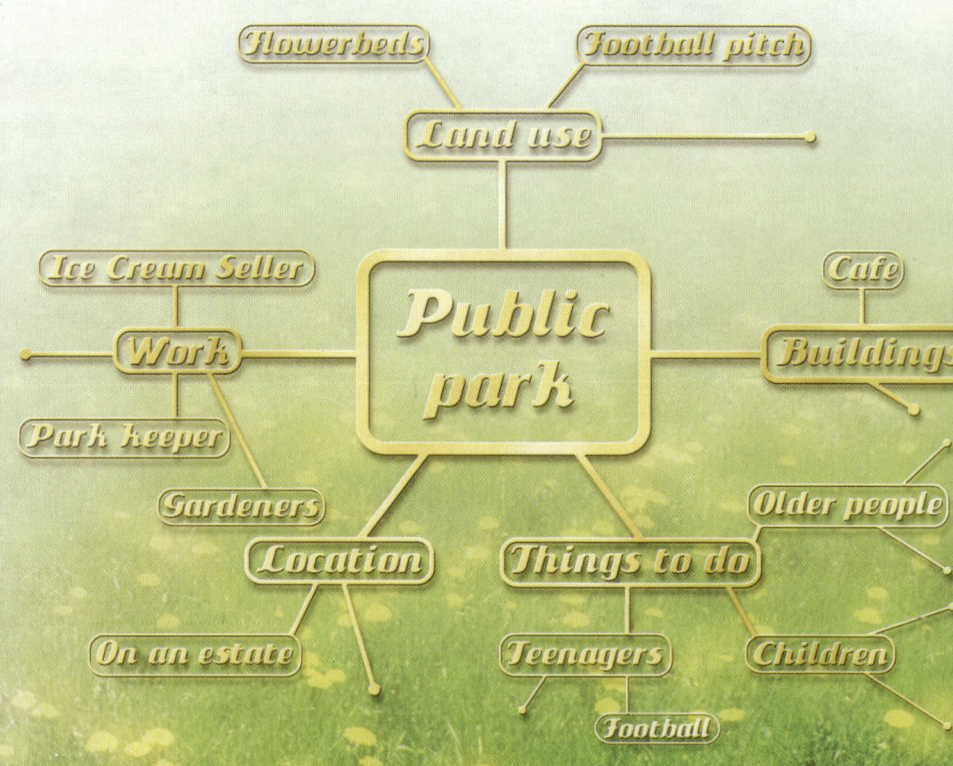

Activities

1. Name three examples of local parks in your area.

2. Complete a copy of the concept map above to describe a local park you know well.

3. Draw a similar concept map for a National Park, using the photographs on the previous pages.

4. How are National Parks and public parks: **a** similar, and **b** different

How to draw a mind map

a Start with a central theme that you want to investigate, in this case either public parks or National Parks.
b Add on the main ideas that spring to mind as being part of the theme. These ideas form main branches leading away from the central theme.
c Develop each of the ideas, dividing as necessary as you think of points you want to add.
d You do not have to finish one branch before you add things to another branch – just note down your ideas as they come to you.
e Use a big piece of paper and colours, illustrate your ideas with pictures.

86 INVESTIGATING GEOGRAPHY A

Activities

5 The statements listed below could be characteristics of three types of park – a public park (Figure 5.7), a National Park (Figures 5.1–5.6), and a third type of park, a **theme park** (Figure 5.9).

- Decide which characteristic can be matched to one or more types of park.
- Work in a group to discuss every statement. Decide which characteristic matches each park; it is possible that all three parks have the same characteristic.
- Record your decisions as a table.

Which of the three types of park are the most likely to:

1 charge a fee to get in
2 charge a fee to park your car
3 provide a habitat for wildlife
4 have activities for small children
5 provide a full family day out
6 be within walking distance of your house
7 have a burger outlet
8 have well kept flower gardens
9 provide new activities each year
10 suffer from vandalism
11 be a place you only go rarely
12 attract people from a wide area
13 have people who live and work there
14 be owned by lots of different people
15 be owned by the local authority
16 cause annoyance to local residents
17 employ people to look after the park
18 be educational
19 offer opportunities for outdoor activities
20 be advertised on TV

Remember

There are no completely right answers to activities like this – so your reasoning is very important.

If you finish quickly try to write one more statement for each type of park.

When you have finished your discussions, prepare your feedback for the rest of the class. You can use the speaking frames below to help you if you like.

'One statement we found easy to place was ..... because .....'

'One statement we argued about was ..... because .....'

'We found it difficult to place the statement about ..... because .....'

◁ Figure 5.9 A theme park

5 National Parks 87

Where are the National Parks in England and Wales?

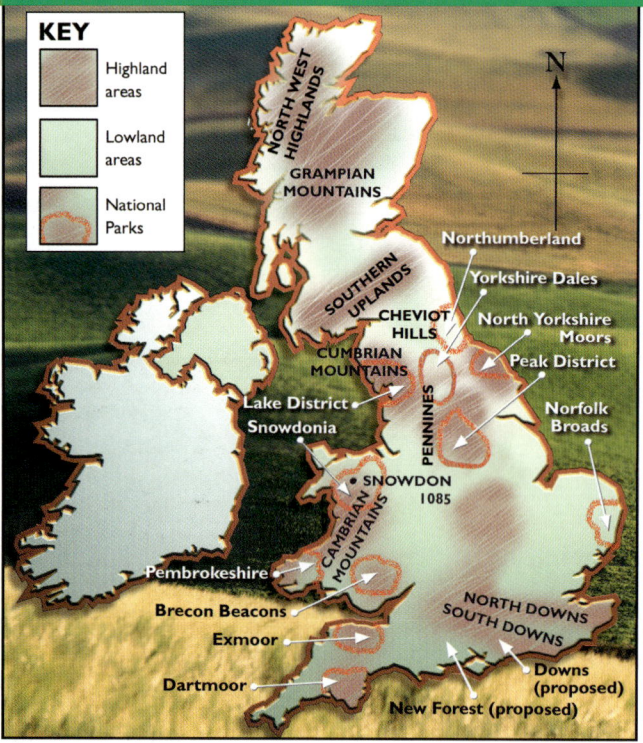

△ **Figure 5.10** Location of the National Parks and relief of England and Wales

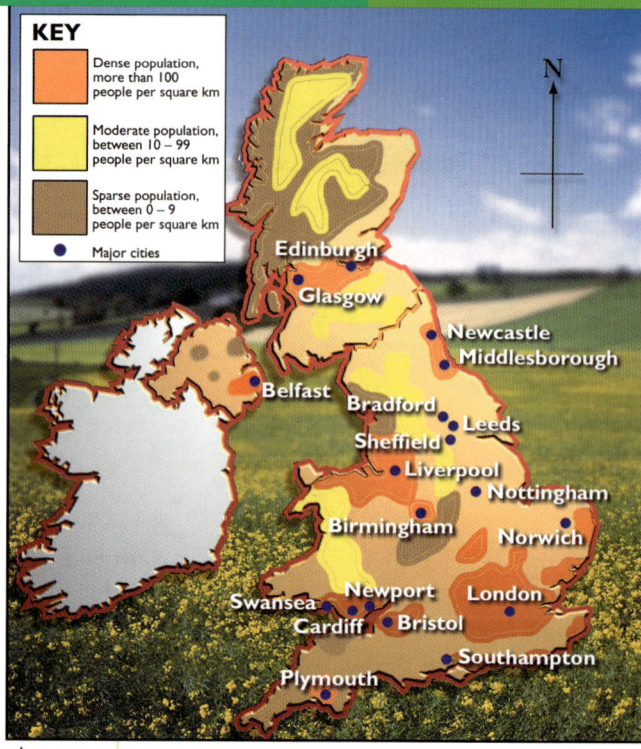

△ **Figure 5.11** Population distribution in England and Wales

An Act of Parliament in 1949 created National Parks in England and Wales. The aim was to protect the countryside and preserve it for future generations to enjoy. Rapid urban growth and increasing demands for water, farming and military use threatened many areas. Each of the National Parks had its own planning authority which worked with landowners to follow guidance to preserve the landscape and wildlife yet provide improved access for visitors. The park authorities tried to make sure that a local economy could continue to support local communities.

Activities

1 Use the maps to decide whether the statements below are True, False or whether there is not enough evidence to tell.
- All the parks are in highland areas.
- The parks are near large urban areas.
- The National Parks have a high population density.
- There are two parks within 100 km of London.
- Northumberland will be the least visited National Park.
- The Peak District will have the highest number of people living nearby.
- There are no large urban areas in National Parks.
- The National Park with the highest mountain is Snowdonia.
- National Parks cover approximately 10% of the area of England and Wales.

2 Which of the following statements do you agree with and why?

'National Parks are in hilly areas because hilly areas tend to be more beautiful so are worth preserving.'

'National Parks tend to be in hilly areas because very few people can live there as it is difficult to make a living there so they are not as damaged as other parts of the country.'

88 INVESTIGATING GEOGRAPHY A

What is the Peak District National Park Like?

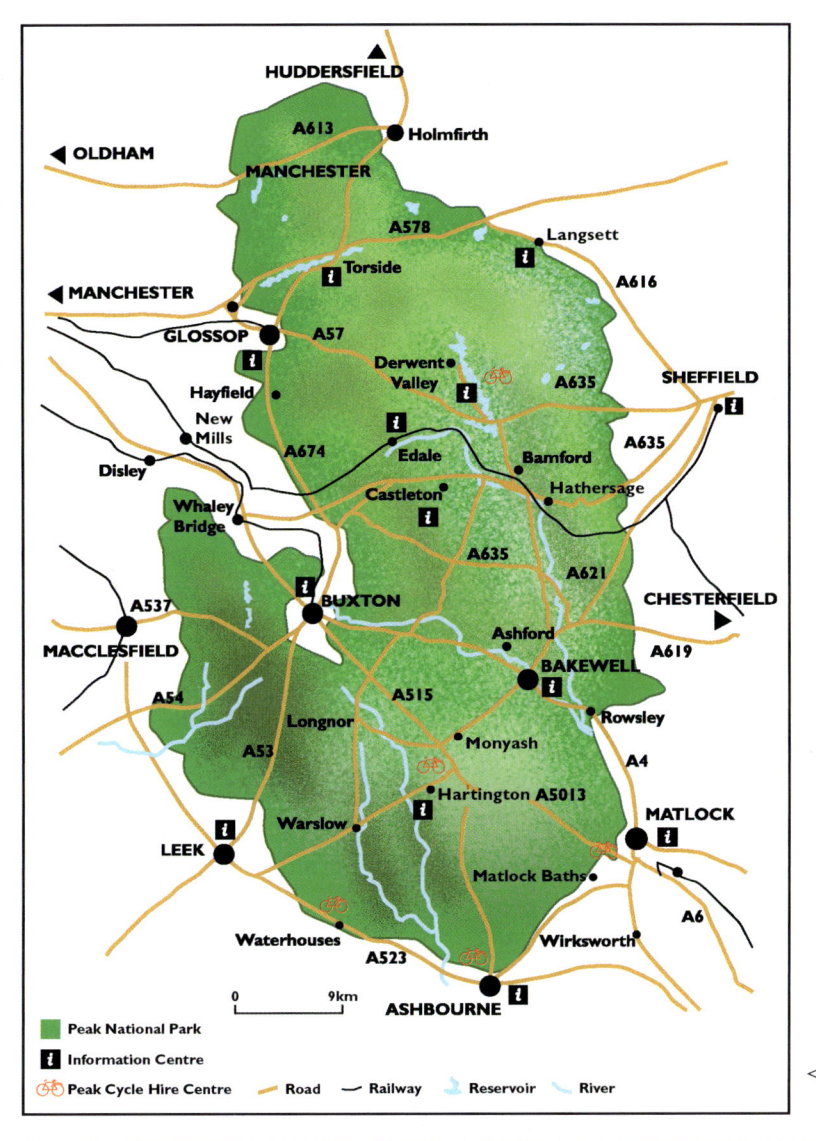

FACT FILE: PEAK DISTRICT

Width ...
Length ...
Area of the park ...
Population 38 100
Population density ...
Nearby cities ...

Number of visitors
22 million/year
Average amount spent
£6/person/day
Income from tourism ...
Names of villages ...

Honeypot sites
Castleton, Bakewell

Activities available ...

Area of moorland 35%
Land owners
National Trust 5%
Forestry Commission 1%
Water Companies 14%
National Park 2%
Private 78%

Castleton is a main **honeypot site** in the Peak District; it attracts many visitors who come to visit the caverns formed in the limestone, shop in the many tourist shops in the village, eat in the tea rooms and cafes, visit Peveril Castle, walk along the many footpaths or just wander around the pretty village.

◁ Figure 5.12 Peak District

◁ Figure 5.13 Castleton

Activities

Foundation

3 Complete a copy of the fact file using information from the map of the Peak District. Use photos showing some of the tourist activities available that bring money into the area; for example, buying food in cafes, buying souvenirs and paying entrance fees.

Target

4 Design and produce a brochure to introduce a visitor to the Peak District.

Extension

5 Explain why Castleton has become a honeypot location.

5 National Parks

How do people make a living in the Peak District?

Figure 5.14 An OS extract showing the Castleton Area from OS Outdoor Leisure 1:25 000

The map shows a small section of the Peak District National Park; this part is in Derbyshire. 22 million people visit the Peak District every year, either for day trips or to stay for a holiday. But there are thousands of people who live and work in the Peak District. There are restrictions about the type of economic activity that can be developed in a National Park. This can mean that fewer jobs are available for local people.

90 INVESTIGATING GEOGRAPHY A

Activities

1 a Using map evidence make a list of the jobs that you can find on the OS map. Give a 6-figure grid reference for each one that you find. For example:

Farm work at 143835, ... at 167834 and ..... at 152831.

b Now classify all the jobs you have found into groups.

c Describe how you arrived at the job groups.

d Suggest why this area has this range of jobs.

2 Draw a graph to show these statistics of jobs in the Peak District:

services	11 000 people
manufacturing	3 500 people
agriculture	2 000 people
quarrying	1 400 people

3 Do the jobs you found on the map reflect the proportions in your graph?

4 Can you think of any problems that might be caused by so many people relying on tourism for their income?

5 Suggest five other jobs which could be encouraged in this area. Give a reason why each job would be suitable for a National Park.

▸ Practise your map skills

6 Figures 5.2 and 5.5 were taken from points on the OS map. The grid references for these photographs are 150826 and 155834.

a Decide where each photograph was taken from.

b Which direction was the camera facing for each photograph?

c Figure 5.13 was also taken in this area. Suggest a grid reference from where this might have been taken. Give a reason for your answer.

7 How far is Hope from Castleton:
a in a straight line?
b along the road?

8 Estimate the area of:
a Castleton Village
b the quarry.

9 Estimate how long it would take you to walk from Castleton village to Hollins Cross. A comfortable walking pace is 4 km/hour. Explain how you worked out your answer.

10 Which grid square contains the higher point 1382 or 1384? Now say which of the two squares has the steeper land and explain how you know.

11 What happens to the contours if you walk west from Castleton village towards Speedwell Cavern? What would it feel like to walk this route?

12 How is Hollins Cross (136845) shown as a high point?

13 How can you tell *from the map* that Castleton is a popular tourist village?

14 Draw a sketch map based on the OS extract to show the tourist attractions in and around Castleton. Either use the OS tourist symbols or design your own set of tourist symbols for the map.

5 National Parks

How would you spend a day in the Peak District?

A family of two adults, a son aged 10 and a daughter aged 12, who like outdoor activities, are going on a day trip to the Castleton area. They only want to spend £25 in total.

Activities

Use the map from page 90 and Figure 5.15 on the right to plan a suitable day out for them.

Remember

Think about ways they could keep the cost down! Not all activities in National Parks cost money! If there are any things you think they might want, available in the area, but not on the list, ask your teacher for a guide price.

△ **Figure 5.15** Price list

- Ice creams — £1 each
- Fish & chips — £3.50 per person
- Crisps — 30p
- Apple — 25p
- Can of pop — 60p
- Entry to cavern — £5 adult, £3.50 child
- Childrens souvenirs — from 50p
- Castle entrance fee — £1.50 adult, 50p child
- Postcard — 20p
- Parking in village car park — £3 per day
- Cup of tea/coffee — £1
- Book of walks around Castleton — £3.50

A suggested way to attempt this task.

- Five minutes to think about any questions or extra prices you want.
- Make a list of ideas from the map.
- Think about how much time would be needed and the cost of each activity.
- Suggest a list of appropriate activities for the family.
- Plan out a timeline for the day.
- Give grid references from the map for the activities you are suggesting.
- List what the family would need to bring with them.
- Explain the reasoning behind your suggestions.

You could even offer alternative suggestions depending on the weather!

Presenting your work

Decide the best way to present your ideas for the family. For example, a piece of writing or perhaps a letter to the family? Would a mind map be a good way to get lots of information in a small space? Perhaps a table with timings and costs would suit some people? An annotated sketch based on one of the photographs might help make things clearer.

What services are available in a National Park Village?

Castleton has a population of 623 people. Sheffield is 20 km and Buxton is 12 km away. There is a local bus service.

Services available for the residents of Castleton

Grocer	3 general stores selling range of foods
Butcher	Nearest shop is in Hope
Baker	Nearest shop is in Hathersage
Greengrocer	Mobile shop visits once per week
Medical centre and chemist	Chemist in Hathersage. Medical centre in Hope
Post Office	In the village
School	Primary school in village, secondary in Hope
Police	Police house in the village, station at Hathersage
Church	C of E and Methodist churches in the village
Library	Mobile library visits once per week
Petrol	Available in the village

Services for visitors to Castleton

B&B/Guest House	7
Hotels	4
Camping/caravan sites	4 (includes camping barn)
Youth hostels	1
Tourist shops/souvenirs	Numerous
Cafes	6
Information centre	1

There are also 6 pubs and a fish and chip shop which benefit both local residents and visitors.

▷ **Figure 5.16** Services in Castleton
Source: www.peakdistrict.org

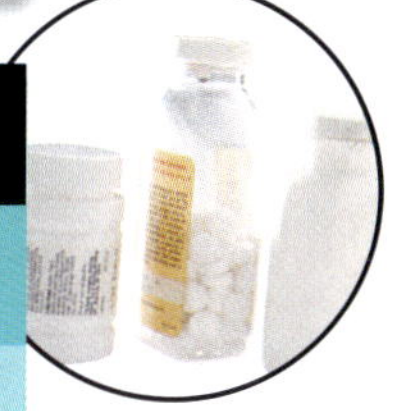

Activities

Foundation

1 What everyday things would you be able to buy in Castleton?

2 Use the OS extract, page 90, to estimate how far residents would have to travel to see the doctor and pick up a prescription.

3 Suggest where the nearest supermarket would be (use Figure 5.12).

Target

4 With a partner make a list of the problems there might be for these residents in Castleton:
- a teenager
- a retired person with no car
- a car owner who works in Sheffield.

5 Give some reasons why people still want to live in villages like Castleton.

Extension

6 a Why do the residents of Castleton have to travel to get the services they need?
b Why is this a problem for some?

7 Suggest how the services in Castleton could be improved.

8 Why are the services in Castleton likely to suffer if there was another outbreak of foot and mouth disease?

5 National Parks

What are national parks like elsewhere?

KEY	
NHS	National Historic Site
NHP	National Historic Park
NM	National Monument
NP	National Park
NPRES	National Preserve
NRA	National Recreation Area
NS	National Seashore

The first National Parks were in the USA. During the 19th century an artist called George Catlin became worried at the way the country was developing. He thought that the Indian heritage and the unspoilt landscape were in danger of disappearing. He became the driving force behind the creation of the first National Parks. In 1872 Yellowstone in Wyoming became the world's first national park. Yosemite followed in 1900.

A national authority, the USA National Parks Service, was set up to look after the increasing number of parks, historical monuments and sites that have since been designated. By 1999 there were 379 locations. This included places as diverse as the arctic wildernesses of Alaska, volcanoes in Hawaii and the Statue of Liberty in New York.

△ **Figure 5.17** National Parks and sites in California

Activities

1 Study Figure 5.17. Write five statements about the type and location of National Parks in California.

2 Use Figures 5.10 and 5.17 and an atlas to complete the comparisons table, Figure 5.18, comparing National Parks in England and California.

3 How are National Parks in England and California:
a similar
b different?

Feature	England	California
Population		
Area		
Number of parks		
Location of the National Parks		
Type of landscapes/relief		
Access to the National Parks		
Cities and urban areas within 50km		

▷ **Figure 5.18** Comparisons table

94 INVESTIGATING GEOGRAPHY A

What is Yosemite National Park like?

Activities

Read this page, which gives a range of information about Yosemite National Park.

1. What does each source of information describe?

2. Would you like to visit Yosemite? Why?

3. Go to the Hodder website and follow the links to the sites about Yosemite. Make a list of ten pieces of extra information about the National Park.

4. Draw a sketch of photograph 5.20 and annotate the main landscape features.

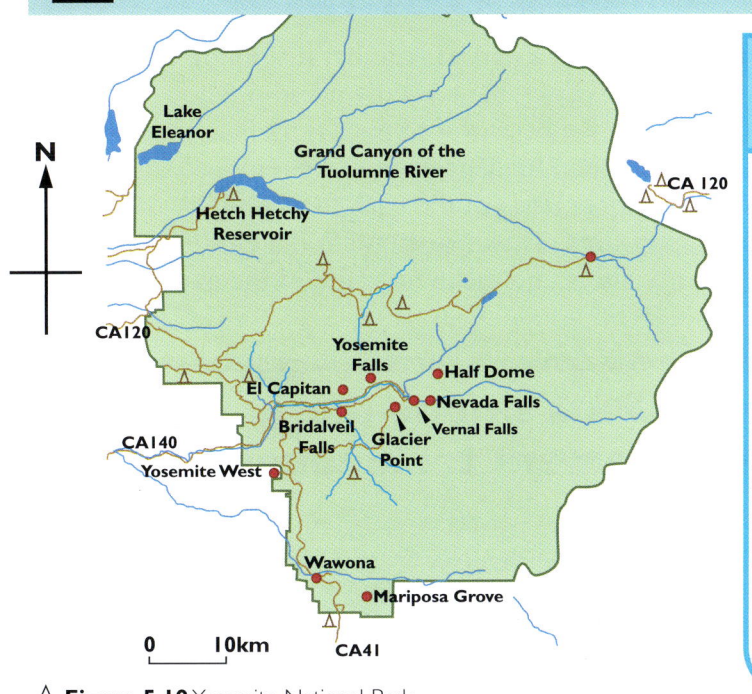

△ **Figure 5.19** Yosemite National Park

FACT FILE: YOSEMITE

Location California, Sierra Nevada
Approx area 760 thousand acres
Wildlife Bears, mountain lions, giant sequoias
Special features Waterfalls, lakes
Numbers of tourists 4 million per year
Weather Winter – snowy with temperatures between –5° and +10° Celsius
Summer – dry with many days reaching 30° Celsius
Entry fee $20 per car/week
Transport 4 entrances to the park. Free shuttle bus in Yosemite Valley

Background to Yosemite

Yosemite was made a National Park in 1890 and has spectacular mountain and valley scenery. Groves of giant sequoias, the world's largest living things, thrive there. Highlights of the park include Yosemite Valley with its high cliffs and waterfalls, sub-alpine meadows at Tuolumne and the Hetch Hetchy reservoir. It became a World Heritage Site in 1984.

▷ **Figure 5.20** Photo of Mirror Lake, Yosemite Valley

❯ Facilities for tourists

- Visitor Centre
- Yosemite Museum
- Tent cabins for rent – $48 per night
- Luxury hotel accommodation – $318 per night
- High Sierra camps in the wilderness – so popular that places are allocated by lottery
- 13 camp sites
- Biking – tours and hiring of bikes
- Bird watching – accompanied tours
- Climbing – ropes are put on the most popular steep climbs to pull yourself up.
- Swimming – in the ice-cold rivers
- Canoes for hire
- Stargazing – after-dark lectures
- Educational programmes for schools and universities
- Horse Riding – accompanied treks and rides
- Wildlife viewing – look out for the bears before they see you!

5 National Parks 95

What conflicts exist In Yosemite?

For thousands of years the area we know as Yosemite National Park was lived in by grizzly bears, black bears and mountain lions, as well as native American people. In the 1840s tourists started to arrive and now over 4 million people a year visit the park. The grizzly bears have all gone, as have the native Americans. The Hetch Hetchy Valley, which was similar to the famous Yosemite Valley, has since been flooded to create a **reservoir** to supply San Francisco.

If you go down to the woods today ...

Most of the tourists who come to Yosemite make their way to the tourist village in Yosemite Valley. Black bears are attracted to the valley by the food that the tourists bring and the rubbish they leave. The bears have become dependent on this food supply. They use their great strength and intelligence to get hold of it. They will trash a car for a carrier bag that just might contain food! They have even worked out how to get into the bear-proof bins. Bears that have these criminal tendencies must be removed to more remote parts of the park for the safety of the visitors. This is just one of the **conflicts** between visitors and the natural life of the parks.

Spring in Yosemite National Park brings more visitors and new bear management techniques

△ **Figure 5.21** Car-breaking bear.

Spring has arrived in the park bringing black bears out from hibernation and visitors to Yosemite National Park. Park staff are prepared with new ideas and techniques to improve the health of the bears whilst reducing bear-related incidents and property damage.

Wildlife staff will increase the emphasis on scaring or 'hazing' bears by such means as noise makers and rubber bullets to chase bears out of campgrounds and public areas. The intent of hazing is to scare the bear, not to harm it. The bears should soon learn to avoid people, developed areas and human food.

Park biologists will be looking for bear hair left on cars that bears have broken into. The biologists can then use DNA testing to work out which bears still climb into vehicles in search of food.

The bear management scheme has been successful since its start in 1998. Between 1998 and 2000 there was a 59% decrease in bear incidents (from 1590 to 654) and an 81% decrease in the amount of property damage caused by bears (down from $659,009 to $126,192). No new adult bears have taken up residence in developed areas, nor have they become food conditioned or habituated to humans.

If bear-human conflict is to be eliminated completely then public co-operation is vital. Park visitors can help by keeping a clean camp, disposing of rubbish properly, and by storing all food and scented items only in the food storage lockers provided in the campgrounds and parking lots. These items should never be stored in vehicles. Bear sightings can be reported to the Save-A-Bear hotline.

Ultimately park visitors are responsible for storing their food properly and saving the lives of bears. Yosemite National Park asks for the public's help in returning the bears to the wild.

△ **Figure 5.22** Extract from www.nps.gov.yose

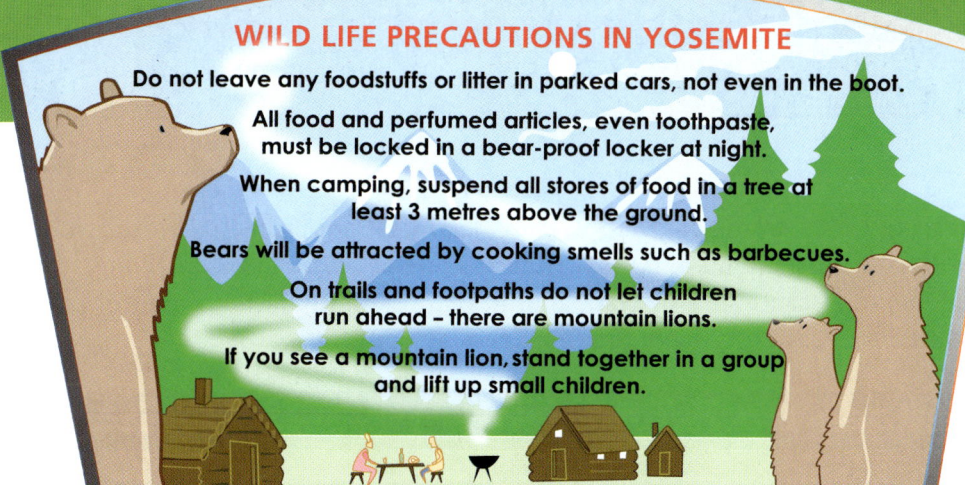

▷ Figure 5.23

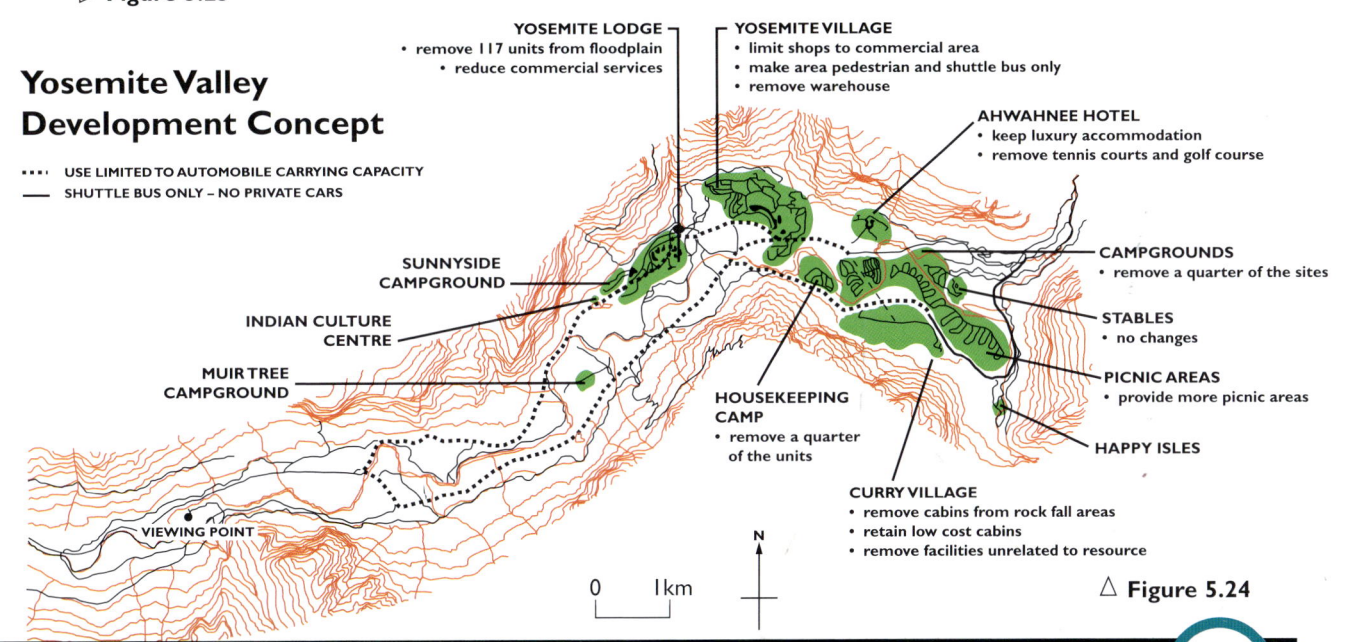

WILD LIFE PRECAUTIONS IN YOSEMITE

Do not leave any foodstuffs or litter in parked cars, not even in the boot.

All food and perfumed articles, even toothpaste, must be locked in a bear-proof locker at night.

When camping, suspend all stores of food in a tree at least 3 metres above the ground.

Bears will be attracted by cooking smells such as barbecues.

On trails and footpaths do not let children run ahead – there are mountain lions.

If you see a mountain lion, stand together in a group and lift up small children.

Yosemite Valley Development Concept

•••• USE LIMITED TO AUTOMOBILE CARRYING CAPACITY
— SHUTTLE BUS ONLY – NO PRIVATE CARS

YOSEMITE LODGE
- remove 117 units from floodplain
- reduce commercial services

YOSEMITE VILLAGE
- limit shops to commercial area
- make area pedestrian and shuttle bus only
- remove warehouse

AHWAHNEE HOTEL
- keep luxury accommodation
- remove tennis courts and golf course

SUNNYSIDE CAMPGROUND

INDIAN CULTURE CENTRE

MUIR TREE CAMPGROUND

CAMPGROUNDS
- remove a quarter of the sites

STABLES
- no changes

PICNIC AREAS
- provide more picnic areas

HAPPY ISLES

HOUSEKEEPING CAMP
- remove a quarter of the units

CURRY VILLAGE
- remove cabins from rock fall areas
- retain low cost cabins
- remove facilities unrelated to resource

VIEWING POINT

0   1km   N

△ Figure 5.24

Activities

Foundation

1 Look at Figure 5.24. Make a list of the changes that are suggested for the valley. Why do you think they are making the changes? Choose three and say how you think the change will reduce conflict in the valley.

2 Why do you think that the Park Authorities have allowed this level of development within the National Park?

Target

3 How could the Park Management and visitors help reduce the impact on bears?
- What could they do?
- Why would they do this?
- How will they know they have been successful?

4 Design a poster to ensure that visitors to the park take the bear problem seriously.

Extension

5 Check on the Yosemite website: www.nps.gov.yose to find out the most recent number of bear incidents.

6 Draw a graph using any figures you find and the ones in the article. Comment on your findings.

5 National Parks 97

What are World Heritage sites?

World Heritage sites are places that people have agreed have outstanding universal value. There are many different types of place that have been identified and currently there are 690 sites that are protected worldwide. Once they are on the list no one can change them in any way; they should look the same for many generations to come.

How does a place become a World Heritage site?

The government of the country where the site is located puts an application to the World Heritage Committee and the 21 members of this group then have to consider the site. Is it a unique geological formation? Is it an important historical site? Is the site in need of protection and preservation? If we do nothing to preserve these sites they could easily disappear like most of the seven wonders of the Ancient World.

Country	Site	Country	Site
Ecuador	Galapagos Islands	Italy	Venice and lagoon
Egypt	Pyramids, Giza	Italy	Pompeii
Kenya	Mt Kenya NP	USA	Yosemite NP
Ghana	Forts and castles, Accra	USA	Statue of Liberty, New York
South Africa	Robben Island	USA	Hawaii volcanoes
Tanzania	Zanzibar, stone town	Brazil	Brasilia
Austria	Town centre, Salzburg	Cuba	Old Havana
Canada	Rocky Mountain parks	Australia	Great Barrier Reef
France	Loire Valley	China	Great Wall
Germany	Cologne Cathedral	India	Taj Mahal
Greece	Acropolis, Athens	Japan	Hiroshima peace memorial
UK	Ironbridge Gorge	Nepal	Mount Everest
UK	Stonehenge	Jordan	Petra

△ **Figure 5.25** A selection of World Heritage sites

Activities

1 With a partner sort the sites listed above into three or four groups of your choosing. First, think of three questions that you would like to ask to help you with this task.

After you have sorted the list into groups, prepare answers to the following questions so that you can explain to the rest of the class how you sorted the sites.

a Which groupings did you decide on?
b How did the questions you asked help you?
c Would any other information have been useful?
d Think of one question that you should have asked.

2 Mark all the sites which are listed here onto a blank world map. Use an atlas to identify the countries. Design a key to show the different types of site.

ICT activity

Visit the website of the World Heritage sites and complete the following tasks:
www.unesco.org/whc/nwhc/pages/sites/main.htm

a Check the current number of World Heritage sites against the 690 when this book was written.
b Find out which country has most sites.
c How many sites are in the UK and which is the closest to where you live?
d Move onto the 'kids' section of the website and take a virtual tour of one of the sites: **www.unesco.org/whc/nwhc/pages/kids/**
e Write a postcard home as if you had really visited the site.

Future World Heritage sites?

△ **Figure 5.26** Castleton and the caverns, Peak District, UK

△ **Figure 5.27** Northumberland Coast, UK

Activities

3 Either for a place you know, or for one of the places shown in the photos on this page, produce a bid to explain why you think the place should become a World Heritage site.
Choose from the following media to present your bid:
- Powerpoint presentation - Maximum 3 slides
- Poster
- Annotated photo or sketch.

◁ **Figure 5.28** Golden Gate Bridge, San Francisco

5 National Parks

Assessment tasks

Background

National Parks have always had the problem of trying to encourage people to visit the countryside whilst needing to conserve the environment for future generations. This leads to conflict. Too many visitors can damage rare plants and **ecosystems**, while over-development of farming or industry can destroy the landscape.

There are significant local populations who live and work in the park. The land in a National Park is not owned by the country; much of it is privately owned or used by water companies, the armed forces or the Forestry Commission. National Park Authorities have a difficult task in balancing everyone's needs.

Farmers
They want to make a living. They need to be sure that any visitors will not damage the land or cause harm to livestock. They also have to pay to maintain footpaths on their land. They may also want to make money from tourists through bed and breakfast or other ways.

Horse riders
They want to use traditional bridle paths, with gates that can be opened from horseback. Some would like to be able to jump over walls and hedges without worrying what was on the other side. Some horse riders would also like to join together to hunt foxes with dogs.

Cement works
They need to quarry limestone which is the basic raw material for cement. They need to be able to process it close to the quarry to cut down on transport costs. After processing, the cement needs to be moved out to the main cities where it will be sold and used. Wider roads would be helpful for all the lorries, and for the introduction of bigger lorries.

Mountain bikers
They want to be able to cycle through the National Parks as the best hills are there. They would like specially designated paths so they don't have to slow down for pedestrians. Stiles also cause them problems and they feel that many could just be left as gaps in the walls or hedges.

Four-wheel drive enthusiasts
They want to view the park whilst negotiating steep slopes and rough terrain in their vehicles. They want to have access to 'green lanes', many of which are now used as footpaths and bridle ways. Groups of drivers like the challenge of driving along these tricky routes.

Local residents
They realise that the area and many of its jobs depend on tourist numbers, but they dislike the fact that some visitors are thoughtless about where they park cars, sometimes blocking drives. They also get fed up with people looking into their homes. Living in a National Park means tight planning regulations and there can be problems if they want to extend their homes. They would like a wider range of services to be available locally.

Hang-gliding enthusiasts
They need access to the hill tops by vehicle so they can get their heavy equipment ready for launch.

Ramblers
They want to be able to walk over all areas whether traditional footpaths exist or not. They feel paths should only be for walkers. They want access to areas of moorland which have been out of bounds for years. They think farmers who block paths should be prosecuted.

△ **Figure 5.29** Who has an interest in the National Parks?

Target tasks

1 Read Figure 5.29. The grid below (Figure 5.30) will help you to work out if there is a conflict between the various groups. The farmers have been checked with the others. Copy and complete the grid for the other seven groups.

	Farmers	Mountain bikers	Hang gliders	Horse riders	4-wheel drivers	Ramblers	Cement works	Local residents
Farmers		💥	💥		💥		💥	
Mountain bikers								
Hang gliders								
Horse riders								
4-wheel drivers								
Ramblers								
Cement works								
Local residents								

△ **Figure 5.30** Conflict matrix

2 Which three groups seem to conflict the most? Can you suggest a reason for this?

3 Suggest three different interested groups who would like to use the National Parks. Would these groups be in conflict with other groups or the natural environment?

4 State five rules a group wanting to use a National Park would have to agree to.
How would these rules help the National Park Authority manage the park?

5 National Parks 101

Assessment tasks

Extension tasks

1 Read Figure 5.29. Think of another group of people who would want to use the National Park and write a similar description of what you think their wishes would be.

2 Use a larger version of Figure 5.31 to map the conflicts that are likely to occur between the groups described in Figure 5.29. Two have been put on for you.
- Use a large sheet of paper.
- Think about use of colour to show links or themes.
- Add small pictures or cartoons.

You should have a very complex diagram when you have finished.

3 Suggest how some of the conflicts you have identified could be solved. Try and answer the questions below to help you.
- Which do you think are the easiest conflicts to tackle?
- Which conflicts do you think cannot be resolved?
- Do you think any of the groups should not be able to use the National Park?
- Are there any new developments that could happen outside the parks that would ease some of the conflicts?

Concept map: Impact of different groups in National Parks

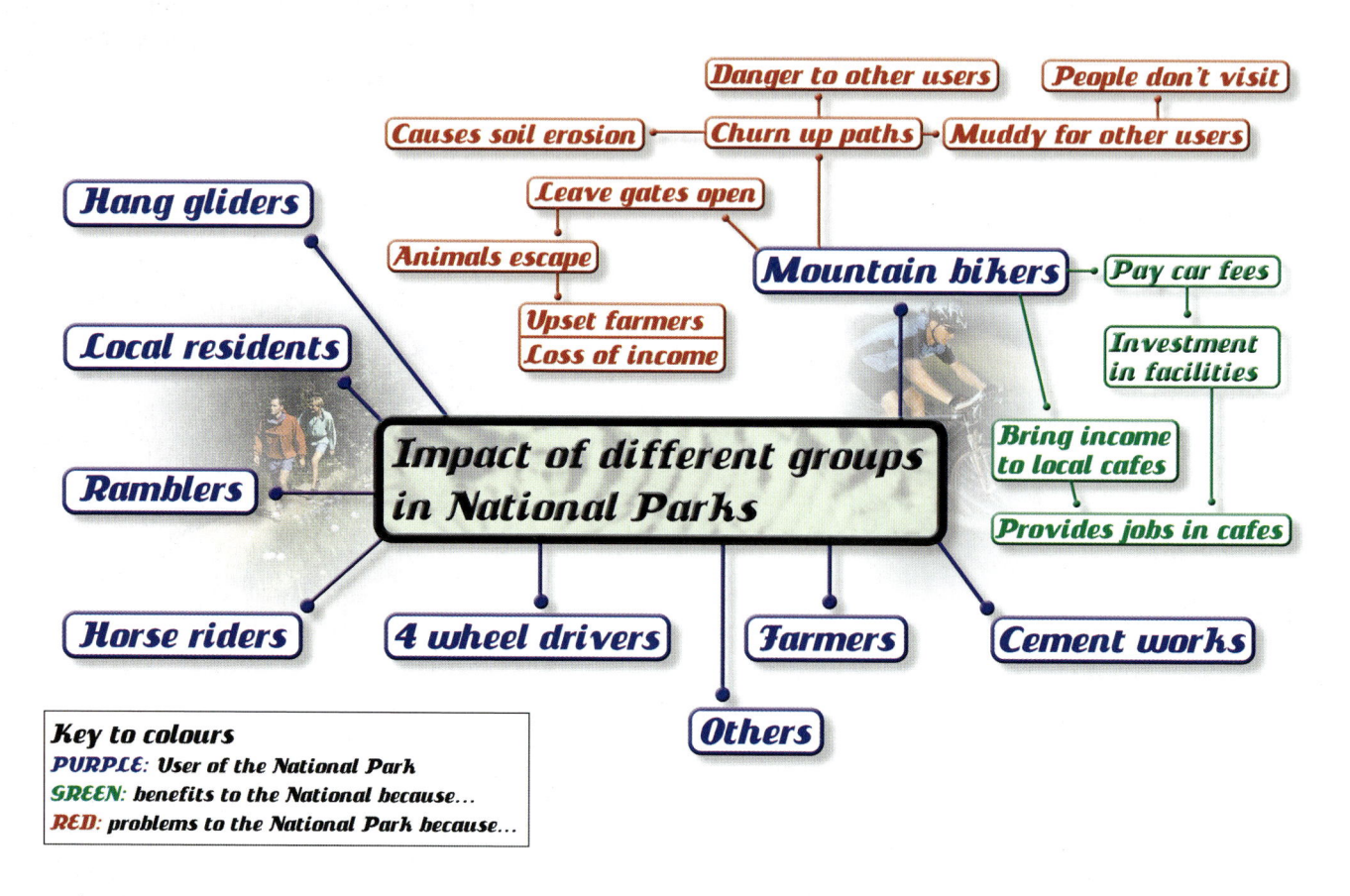

Groups (Users of the National Park): Hang gliders, Local residents, Ramblers, Horse riders, 4 wheel drivers, Farmers, Others, Cement works, Mountain bikers

Problems (red):
- Mountain bikers → Danger to other users
- Mountain bikers → Churn up paths → People don't visit / Muddy for other users
- Causes soil erosion
- Leave gates open → Animals escape → Upset farmers / Loss of income

Benefits (green):
- Mountain bikers → Pay car fees
- Investment in facilities
- Bring income to local cafes
- Provides jobs in cafes

Key to colours
PURPLE: User of the National Park
GREEN: benefits to the National because...
RED: problems to the National Park because...

△ **Figure 5.31** Concept map framework

102 INVESTIGATING GEOGRAPHY A

Review

What have I learnt about National Parks?

Figure 5.32 is a list of words that should be familiar to you after completing the work on National Parks. This exercise will check your understanding of the ideas and terms used.

1	Yosemite	12	horse riders
2	conflict	13	relief
3	Peak district	14	World Heritage site
4	historic site	15	rare plants
5	camping	16	farmer
6	rambling	17	cafe
7	resident	18	theme park
8	conservationist	19	Exmoor
9	park ranger	20	Norfolk Broads
10	fox	21	mountain lions
11	bear		

△ Figure 5.32 National Park words

Activities

1. Start with Group A. Write out the words from Figure 5.32 that make up this group. Decide with a partner which word is the odd one out and why. Give a clear reason for your choice.

2. Work through the other groups, keeping a note of the choice of odd-one-out words and the reasons.

3. Look at the final list of odd-one-out words and the reasons. Are there any common features? If so what?

4. Try to add another word to each of the groups so that the same odd-one-out word is kept.

Group A	3	19	20	
Group B	10	11	21	
Group C	9	17	15	
Group D	8	10	16	
Group E	2	6	16	20
Group F	7	8	10	16
Group G	1	10	11	21
Group H	7	11	17	22
Group I	1	3	13	20
Group J	1	4	14	18

△ Figure 5.33 Word groups

5 National Parks 103

6 Population

Is there a perfect place to live?

▷ Figure 6.1

I live in a place with few other people. I am a farmer and I need plenty of land for my cattle to graze. My family has been in this area for hundreds of years. I like living here. I have everything I need. I sometimes think the world would be a better place if there were fewer people around to spoil it. The people in cities need the countryside or where would they get their food?

I have a very busy life in the place where I live. There are always lots of people around and always lots of things to do. I enjoy being part of a busy place although I get a bit fed up of traffic jams and crammed trains.

I live somewhere that has many new visitors every week. The place I live is very beautiful, but does not have many of the modern things that people take for granted in towns and cities. We all love the fantastic weather and would not swap our home for anywhere in the world. The only thing that I don't like about the visitors is the mess they leave behind and the way they ignore the damage they do to our beautiful environment.

The place we live is never boring. There's always plenty to do. Our home has all that we need, it's comfortable, warm, and has electricity. Why would we need to move? It's perfect! We're lucky I guess, there are plenty of poorer families in the world who have lots of children and can't afford to give them a life like ours.

104 INVESTIGATING GEOGRAPHY A

Figure 6.2

Activities

1 Can you work out where the people in Figure 6.1 live? Choose from the places in Figure 6.2.

2 Give three reasons why you have chosen the picture for each of the people.

3 If you had to choose a second picture for each of the people, which would it be and why?

4 Each of the people has a view on population issues. Write out their opinion and say whether you agree or disagree with it. Explain the reasons for your decision.

5 Where do you live? Describe your home like the people have done in Figure 6.1. Would you move if you had the chance or is it the perfect place for you? Does living there satisfy all your needs?

6 Population

What do you already know about population?

People live in different places for many different reasons. Some can choose to live where they like, but for others, life may not be so easy.

For humans to live anywhere they need certain physical conditions to survive. For example, a climate that is not too hot or cold, a supply of water, a source of food and somewhere to live, or shelter.

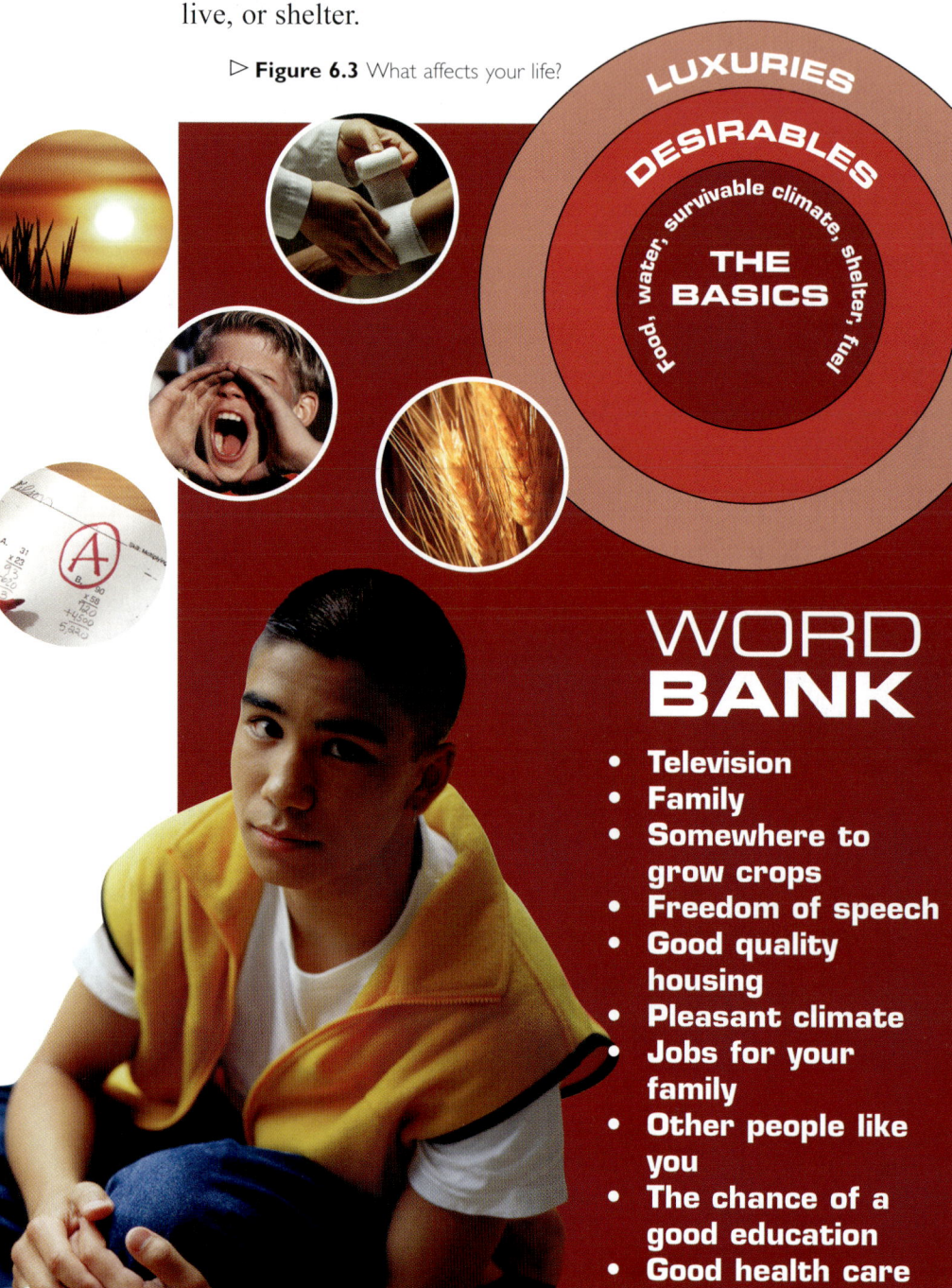

▷ **Figure 6.3** What affects your life?

LUXURIES
DESIRABLES
THE BASICS
Food, water, survivable climate, shelter, fuel

WORD BANK

- Television
- Family
- Somewhere to grow crops
- Freedom of speech
- Good quality housing
- Pleasant climate
- Jobs for your family
- Other people like you
- The chance of a good education
- Good health care

Activities

Let's start with the basics of survival and work our way up to other reasons that control where we live.

1 Make a copy of the large circular diagram (Figure 6.3) or simply draw a table with three columns headed: 'The basics', 'Desirables' and 'Luxuries'.

Now use the word bank to make your personal version of the diagram. Add as many of your own words as possible.

2 Compare what you have done with at least three other people. What are the similarities and differences?

3 Look back at the people in the pictures on pages 104. Choose one group who have a different life to you and do the activity again but through their eyes.
Compare your diagram with the one for this group.

106 INVESTIGATING GEOGRAPHY A

What's the big picture?

Over the next few pages you will be introduced to a lot of new ideas. All of them have some connection with the theme of population. Figure 6.4 shows how some of these ideas are linked. It is called a concept map. All of the ideas below are explained in this chapter, but only here can you see how they all fit together. This will be an important page to look back at when you complete a section to see how any new information you have learned fits in the big picture.

High growth rates lead to high population density.

People are not spread around the world evenly. Crowded areas we call high density.

Birth rates and Death rates control growth. Structure is age & gender shown in population pyramids.

DISTRIBUTION & DENSITY

GROWTH & STRUCTURE

Where there are more natural resources, the population density is normally high.

Migration can lead to changes in structure.

People use natural resources to live. These resources can make certain areas very popular.

POPULATION

Not everyone stays in one place. They move for many different reasons, nearly always to improve their lives.

NATURAL RESOURCES

MIGRATION

People will move to find natural resources.

△ Figure 6.4 Population concept map

What's so important about population?

Some people call population a problem. They believe that there are:
- too many people being born or dying
- too many people in crowded cities and too few in the countryside
- too many people trying to migrate from the poorer parts of the world to the richer parts of the world.

To understand what is really important about population you need to know:
- the way population is changing
- the impact of population growth on the environment
- what could be done.

This chapter, and other parts of this series, will help you with these issues.

6 Population 107

What is population distribution?

△ Mumbai

△ Peruvian Andes

△ **Figure 6.5** World map showing population distribution

Every dot on the world map shows an area where a large amount of people live. The pattern these dots make is called a **distribution**.

So Figure 6.5 shows the population distribution around the world. You can see that some places have more people living in them than others.

There are a number of reasons why there is an uneven distribution of people around the world. They can be put into two groups: *Positive* reasons and *Negative* reasons. These are the reasons that people will use to choose where they live. Each of the positive and negative reasons can be either linked with the natural environment (*Physical Factors*), or the environment created by people (*Human Factors*).

Many areas with large numbers of people living in them have grown up because of these good points, but now people live there for other reasons. For example, in the UK most people live in towns and cities, but why?

▽ **Figure 6.6** Positive and Negative Factors

Activities

1 Use an atlas to name three countries where there are many people shown on the map, Figure 6.5, and three where there are very few people.

2 You are going to create a good place for people to live. To do this you must decide which factors you want the place to have so people will find it easy to live there. Use the list of *Positive* and *Negative* factors in Figure 6.6.

➕ POSITIVE & NEGATIVE FACTORS
➖ But which are which?

- Cold climate
- Flat land
- A good water supply
- A place to work
- Wars and fighting
- Easy to move around
- No natural resources for building or fuel
- A Government that doesn't listen to the people
- Good soils for growing crops
- Clean air and amazing views

108 INVESTIGATING GEOGRAPHY A

What is population density?

When we count the number of people living in a certain area and divide it by the size of the area, we are left with the **population density**; in other words the number of people per square kilometre of land. By looking at Figures 6.7 and 6.8, you can see that population density varies from place to place.

The map opposite shows where people live in the world; the **population distribution**.

▽ **Figure 6.7** Town versus Country

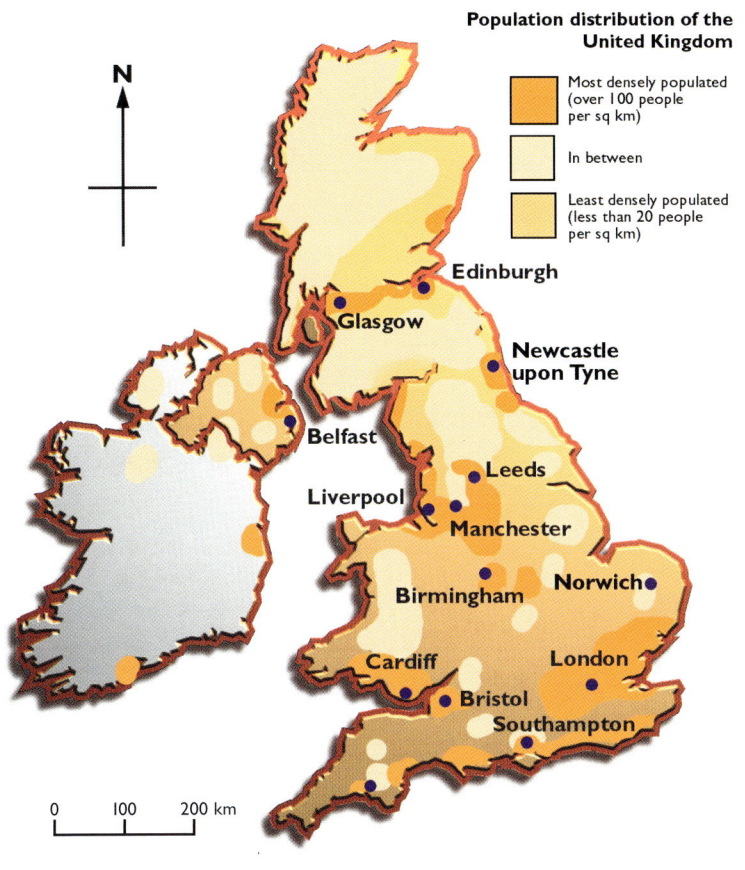

Figure 6.8 UK population distribution and density

Population distribution of the United Kingdom
- Most densely populated (over 100 people per sq km)
- In between
- Least densely populated (less than 20 people per sq km)

Activities

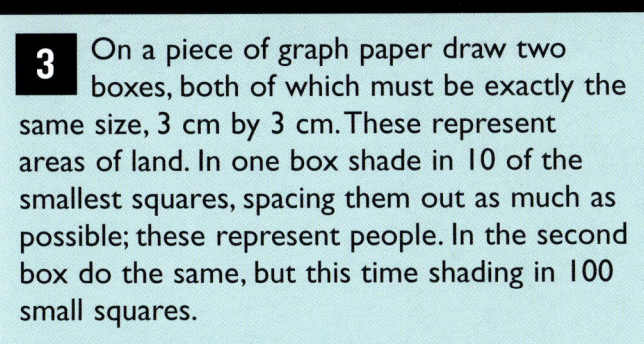

3 On a piece of graph paper draw two boxes, both of which must be exactly the same size, 3 cm by 3 cm. These represent areas of land. In one box shade in 10 of the smallest squares, spacing them out as much as possible; these represent people. In the second box do the same, but this time shading in 100 small squares.

One of your boxes shows an area of high population density, the other, low density. Which is which?

4 The map of the UK, Figure 6.8, shows the population distribution and density in the UK. You can see that most people live in cities like Leeds, Birmingham and London. There are far fewer people in the north and west of Scotland, central Wales and north of England. Find a map of the physical landscape of the UK to work out why this is.

5 Name two parts of the UK that are 'most densely populated' and two parts that are 'least densely populated'. What are your areas like? What are the main similarities and differences?

6 Population   109

What is population growth?

The world's population is growing very quickly. If you want to know how quickly then just visit the POPClocks on this website: www.census.gov/main/www/popclock.html

They give you an idea of the number of new babies being born each minute in the USA and in the world.

Work out how much the population of the world will have increased: by the end of your lesson; by the end of school today; and by this time next week.

Populations increase when the number of new babies born is greater than the number of people dying. The number of babies being born each year is called the **birth rate**. The number of people who die each year is called the **death rate**. Each of these is measured out of every 1 000 of a country's population. People moving into or out of a country can also affect the speed of population increase called its **population growth rate**. The increase in population is greater in poorer countries than in richer countries. They normally have high birth rates.

What is it like to live in these countries with different birth and death rates?

ETHIOPIA
A country in Africa with a population of 58 million people. It covers 1.13 km². People living in this country have a life expectancy of just over 41 years.

FRANCE
This country is in Europe, it has 58 million people living in it. It covers 547 030 km². In this country the age you would be expected to live to would be 78 years old.

ICT activity
Use the following website to build a population profile of different countries. You can also use it to compare countries' statistics.

www.your-nation.com

Births each year per 1 000 people

Deaths each year per 1 000 people

ETHIOPIA 44.69 — FRANCE 11.68

ETHIOPIA 21.25 — FRANCE 9.12

▷ Figure 6.9 Birth rate: Ethiopia and France

◁ Figure 6.10 Death rate: Ethiopia and France

What is population structure?

The number of men, women and children in a country can be shown by looking at a special kind of graph called a **population pyramid**. We can use it to find out about the way a country's population has grown in the past and how it may change in the future. Put very simply, it shows how a country's population can be divided into groups of men and women of different ages.

Look at the two population pyramids for Ethiopia and France, Figure 6.11. They are very different shapes. One has a wide base and a narrow top; the other has a base that is not wider than the rest of the pyramid, which bulges in the middle and then only narrows slowly near the top.

What is the point of studying population pyramids?

A wide base, like in Ethiopia's pyramid, indicates a high birth rate. A very narrow top can indicate a high death rate. Studying the population pyramid of a country gives us a chance to predict how it will look in the future. Birth rates and death rates can change how a country uses its resources. As populations are growing so quickly in some countries, people are finding it difficult to provide everybody with clean water, food, shelter, clothes, schools, hospitals and jobs. So planning for a large bulge in population is important.

ICT links

The USA Census website has a good page where you can create your own population pyramids for any country; have a look at it:
www.census.gov/ipc/www/idbpyr.html

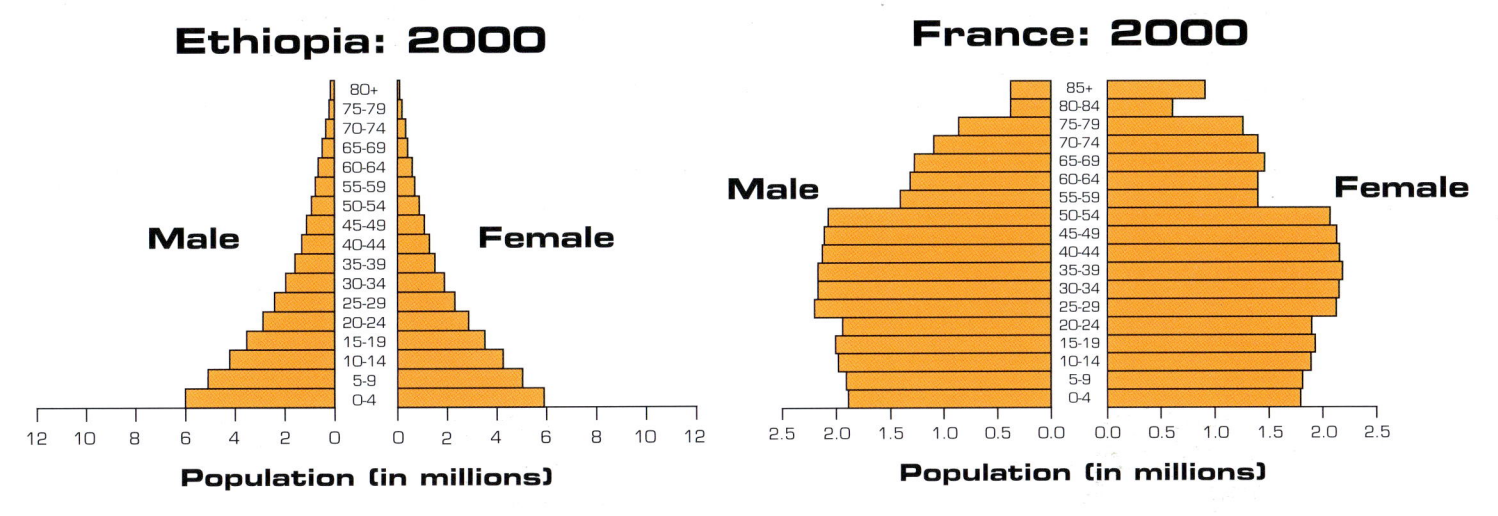

△ **Figure 6.11** Population pyramids: Ethiopia and France

Activities

Foundation

1 Which of the two countries seen on this page has:
a the highest proportion of young people?
b the largest number of old women?

Target

2 Will France or Ethiopia have to look after a large number of older people in the next 30 years?

Extension

3 Explain the link between population growth rates and the shape of the population pyramids for Ethiopia and France.

What is population change?

The main reason for an increase or decrease in population is usually a change in the birth and/or death rate. Geographers use a model, called the **population cycle** or **demographic transition**, to show how birth and death rates change over time. (A model is an idea – things may not happen exactly as the model shows.) The demographic transition model has four stages, each of which is described in Figure 6.12. There are a number of reasons for the changes shown on the graph.

Links to population pyramids

The demographic transition can be linked to population pyramids. Birth rates show at the base of the pyramid while death rates can be seen at the top of the pyramid.

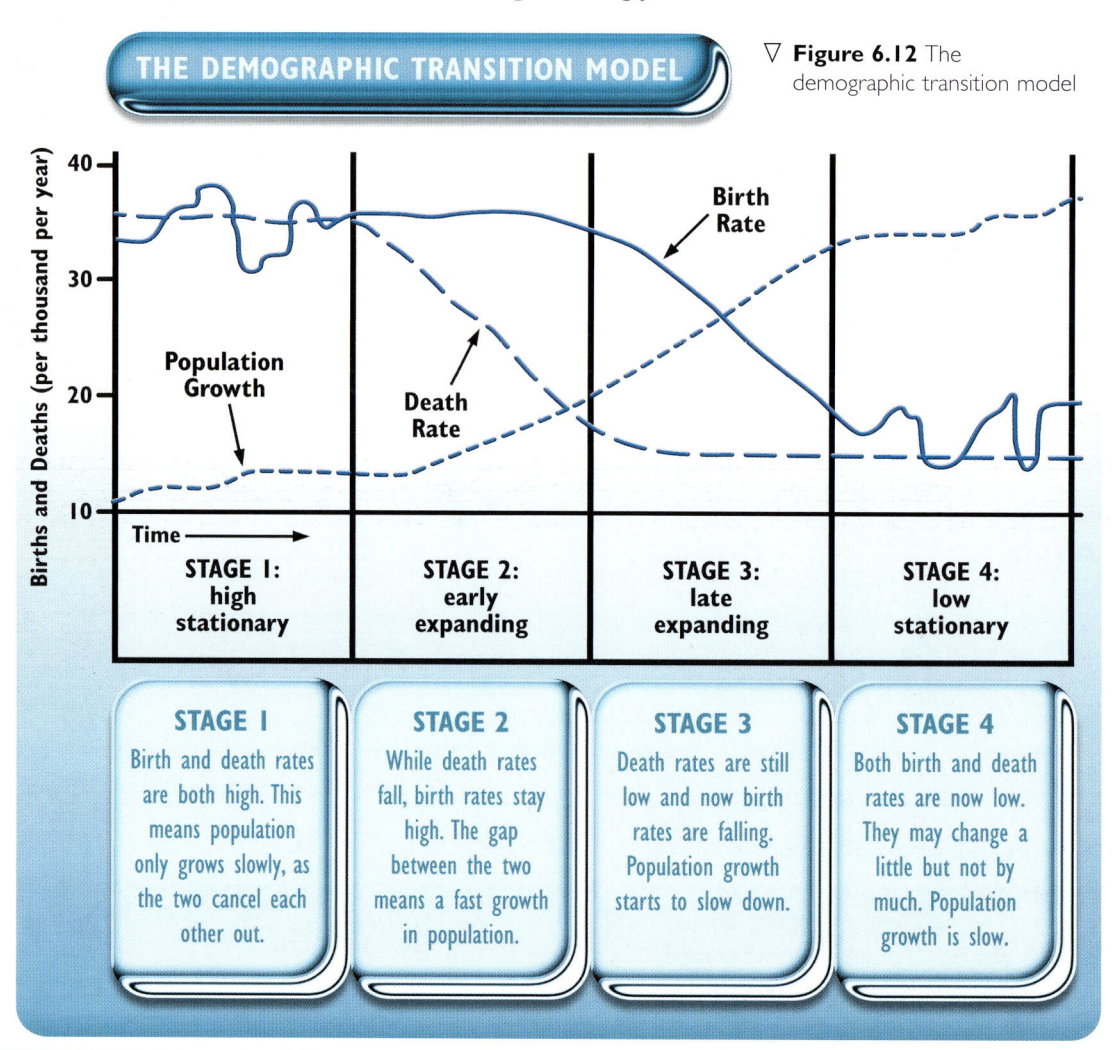

THE DEMOGRAPHIC TRANSITION MODEL

▽ **Figure 6.12** The demographic transition model

STAGE 1: high stationary
STAGE 2: early expanding
STAGE 3: late expanding
STAGE 4: low stationary

STAGE 1
Birth and death rates are both high. This means population only grows slowly, as the two cancel each other out.

STAGE 2
While death rates fall, birth rates stay high. The gap between the two means a fast growth in population.

STAGE 3
Death rates are still low and now birth rates are falling. Population growth starts to slow down.

STAGE 4
Both birth and death rates are now low. They may change a little but not by much. Population growth is slow.

Why do these changes take place?

Death rates begin to fall first as it is often easier for countries to improve diets and/or the way they fight disease than control the number of children people have.

112 INVESTIGATING GEOGRAPHY A

BONJOUR, I am ISABELLE and live in Bordeaux in France. My sister and I live with our parents. They both work all day. Most of my friends only have small families but we all have older relations still alive. I don't think that I will get any more brothers or sisters as our parents could not afford to keep us all.

HELLO, my name is ABDUL and I live in Tanzania in Africa. I have many sisters and brothers and our family grows all the time. Not as many young children die now as in the past because we have new medicines which help them to survive. Medicines also help some of the older people in the village to live longer.

HELLO, my name is RAONI. I live with my sisters and brothers in the Amazon Rainforest. Our parents say that we must all have many children when we grow up because many babies die in our village. There are hardly any old people in my family. My grandfather died last year, he was only 43 years old. We have a very large graveyard here.

HELLO, I am MARIA and I live in Brazil. I have two brothers and a sister. My parents come from a very large family, but they say it is getting too expensive to keep a large family these days. They say that modern medicines and reliable methods of birth control have helped them live longer and limit their family to a smaller but healthier one.

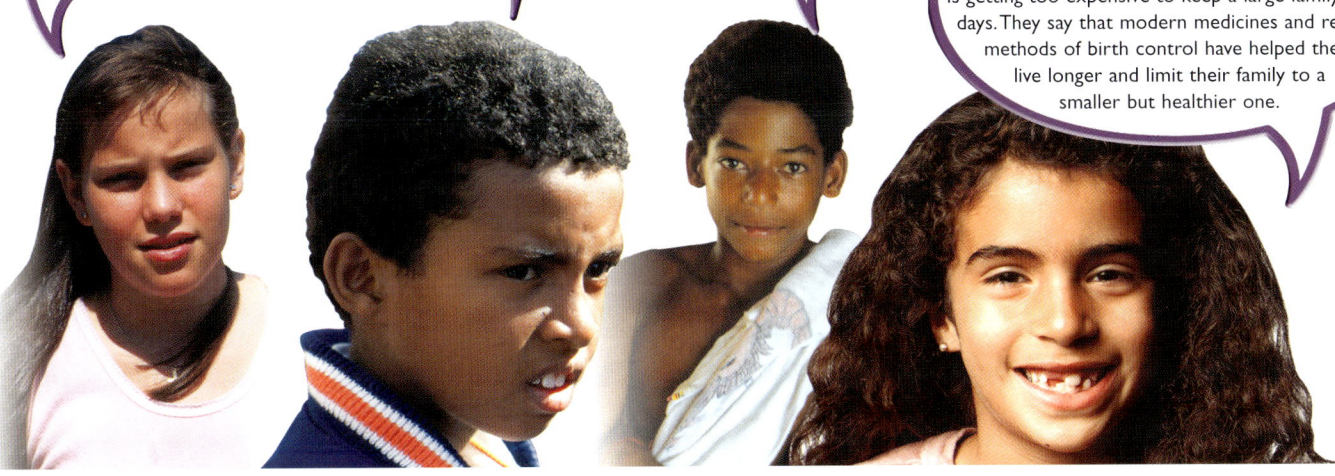

△ **Figure 6.13** Population change and people's lives

Activities

1. Each of the four children above (Figure 6.13) comes from a country at a different stage in the demographic transition (population cycle). Can you find out which stages they belong in?

2. Britain has passed through most of the demographic transition (population cycle). Use the data table (Figure 6.14) to plot the changes in birth rate and death rate that have taken place since 1600.

3. Try to work out where the line showing population growth should go.

4. Finally, explain what factors could have caused the changes you have shown.

Date	Birth Rate	Death Rate
1600	31	30
1650	29	29
1700	30	31
1750	35	30
1800	39	26
1850	34	23
1900	29	18
1950	20	14
2000	12	12

△ **Figure 6.14** The UK's changing population

6 Population 113

What is migration?

While birth and death rates affect population growth, so do the number of people moving into or out of a country. We call this movement of people **migration**. Both examples show migration at different scales. If people move into a country, it is called **immigration**, and if they move out of the country, it is called **emigration**.

Why do people migrate?

There are lots of reasons why people move away from one area to another. We can put these reasons into two groups: **Push factors**, those things about a place that you may not like; and **Pull factors**, things that attract you to an area.

The reasons why people move in MEDCs are often related to their jobs and families. There is more of a choice for people, both in countryside areas and cities.

In LEDCs the factors that make people move are often more a matter of survival. In Mexico, this means that the push and pull factors for people may be very different to those in more wealthy countries, like the UK.

Activities

1. Use the diagram (Figure 6.15) to list Push and Pull factors for both types of country.

2. On a larger copy of the **Venn diagram** opposite (Figure 6.16) classify the factors you have listed. Those that are the same in both types of country go in the middle, while the ones only found in one type go in the side sections.

3. Describe the differences and similarities of Push and Pull factors between MEDCs and LEDCs.

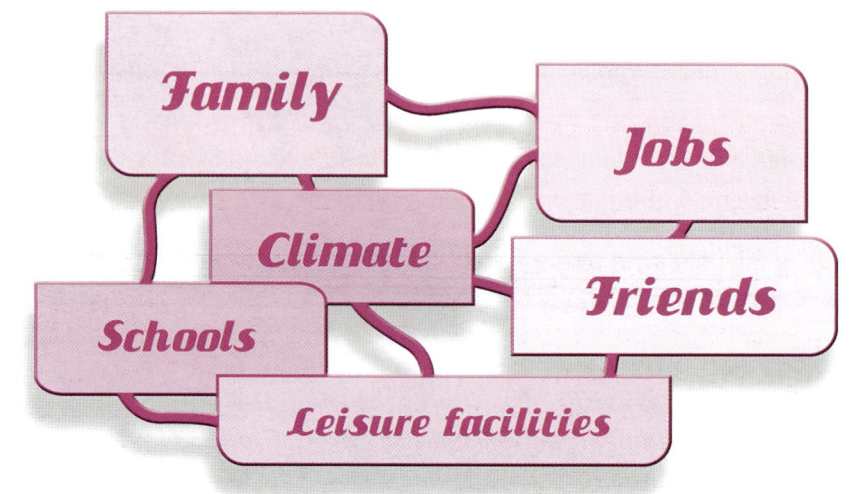

△ **Figure 6.15** Reasons why people move in MEDCs

Factors: Family, Jobs, Climate, Friends, Schools, Leisure facilities

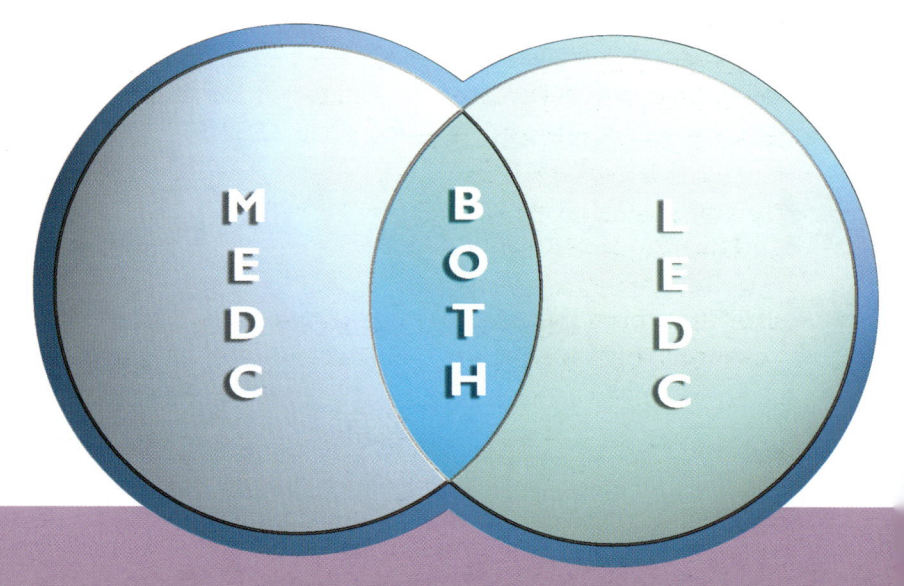

▷ **Figure 6.16** Venn diagram showing Push and Pull factors in MEDCs and LEDCs

(Venn diagram: MEDC | BOTH | LEDC)

114 INVESTIGATING GEOGRAPHY A

Activities

Why did Emilio Sanchez leaves El Dorado?

4 Look at the statements (Figure 6.17) and use any information in them to help you explain why Emilio has decided to leave his village, El Dorado. Use the terms 'Push' and 'Pull' factors to help *classify* your answers.

- El Dorado used to be an important farming centre.
- El Dorado has two shops which sell food and clothes.
- Emilio's family like to watch TV programmes from the USA.
- There are 175 people living in El Dorado and the number keeps falling.
- Emilio is nearly 18 years old.
- Conchita, Emilio's mother, misses having all her family around.
- Emilio's brothers have both left home in search of work.
- El Dorado is 75 miles from Mexico's border with the USA.
- Just like last year, the Sanchez family farm has failed to make much money.
- Emilio has an uncle who works illegally in a factory in the USA. He earns 10 times what Emilio ever could.
- There are more old people in El Dorado than young ones like Emilio.
- Emilio's father, Diego, was killed trying the cross the Rio Grande, the border between the USA and Mexico.
- In Emilio's village there has been a long history of people leaving to find their fortune in the USA. Very few have ever come back, but very few have ever really made their dreams come true in the USA.
- They have a memorial to those who have been killed trying to cross the border.

△ **Figure 6.17** Why did Emilio Sanchez leave El Dorado?

6 Population 115

What is migration?

The effect of migration on the migrants

The reasons that people have for moving between countries can be very strong. The chance of improving their lives is always important. Sometimes the desire to migrate is so powerful that people will take great chances and even risk their lives for the chance to live somewhere they think will give them a better life.

△ Figure 6.19 Ferry unloading at Dover; Forensics inspecting a lorry

Grim find of 58 bodies in lorry exposes smugglers' evil trade

Nick Hopkins, Jeevan Vasagar, Paul Kelso and Andrew Osborn

Although he could not see right inside, the customs officer knew something was terribly wrong the moment he opened the heavy swing doors.

The container on the white Mercedes lorry was a refrigeration unit, yet the air that belched out was warm and smelled putrid.

In the half light, he saw two Chinese men sprawled in front of him, gasping for breath. Behind them in the gloom, the officer saw what a colleague described as a scene "out of a nightmare." Fifty-eight bodies lay haphazardly on the metal floor in between seven crates of tomatoes.

Police suspect the 54 men and four women found dead during the routine inspection at Dover just before midnight on Sunday were illegal entrants from the Fujian province of China, who paid a criminal gang, called snakeheads, thousands of pounds for the chance to start a new life in the UK.

△ Figure 6.18 From the *Guardian*, Tuesday, 20 June, 2000

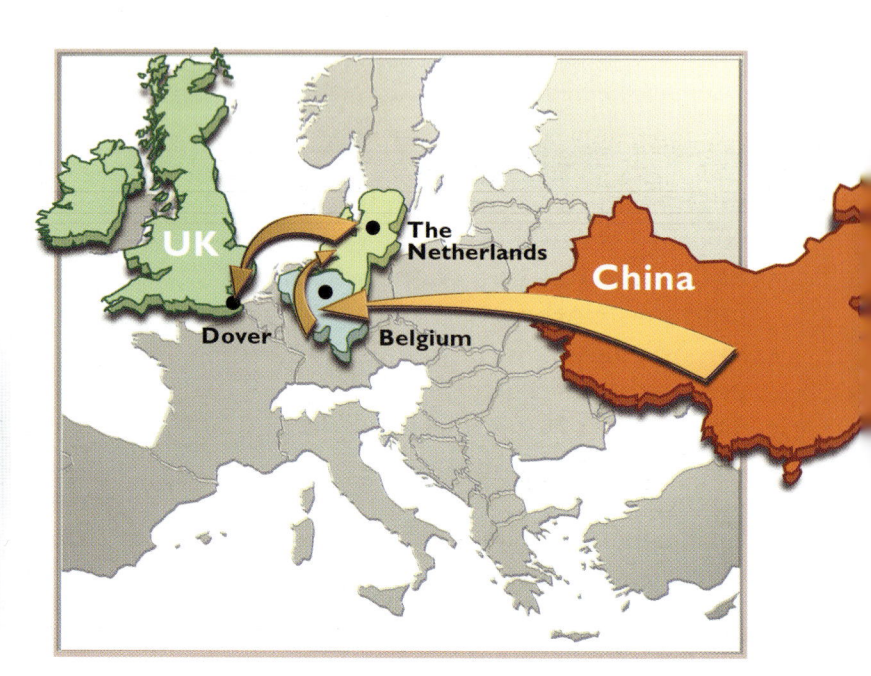

△ Figure 6.20 The route the refugees' lorry took from China to the UK

The newspaper article, Figure 6.18, tells the story of men and women who had tried to get into the UK illegally. They had paid a gang of smugglers to transport them in a lorry from The Netherlands, on a ferry and into England at the port of Dover. There were many risks involved but they wanted to change their lives so much they were willing to take them. Things went very badly wrong for these people.

116 INVESTIGATING GEOGRAPHY A

The effects of migration on the places people move to or from

It is not only the migrants that have their lives affected by moving to another country. The area they move to can change greatly as a result of many new people moving in. This can worry some people who may have got used to their home town the way it has always been. Some people feel that they have been unfairly asked to change their way of life for these immigrants.

Other problems are caused in the areas where people are moving from. Often these are rural areas where the villages are becoming smaller, with fewer young people and skilled workers to continue the traditions of the community.

Dover, no port in a storm for refugees

Vikram Dodd

In the garden of England, a hatred is kindling. Dover is being torn apart by the presence of 700 asylum seekers and 1,400 of the port's 30,000 residents have signed a petition protesting at Kent country council's decision to add £3 to the council tax to pay for the upkeep of the refugees. Sitting in her garden, petition organiser Sheila Farrell rails against the asylum seekers. She is joined by Chris Ryan, a former fisherman, who is appalled by the impact of the newcomers on Dover. "We're trying to do something for the residents and we get called racist," says Mrs Farrell.

Film of the week 'Not One Less'

Peter Preston

This film is about a primary school class deep in rural China. There are no adults left to become teachers, so a 13-year-old girl, Wei, is given the job. The film tells us that a million children a year have to drop out of school in China because of desperate poverty. It reminds us that the pull of the city is draining resources and hope from the countryside in China.

△ **Figure 6.22** From the *Observer*, Sunday, 25 June, 2000

◁ **Figure 6.21** From the *Guardian*, Tuesday, 28 March, 2000

Activities

Foundation

1 What can be the effects of migration on the migrants? Use the information in Figures 6.18 and 6.21. Choose some of the words below to help you explain:

- Death
- No guaranteed jobs
- Exploited by people
- Unwelcome
- Sent home.

Target

2 Why do you think the Chinese immigrants in the first report (Figure 6.18) were willing to take such a risk getting to the UK?

3 Who should be responsible for looking after immigrants arriving in this country?

4 What has happened to many villages in China like the one the immigrants came from, which is similar to the one described in Figure 6.22?

Extension

5 Who do you think is to blame for the disaster that killed the 58 Chinese immigrants in the first report (Figure 6.20)?

6 Are the residents of Dover, described in the second report (Figure 6.21), justified in feeling the way they do toward immigrants?

7 Will the people still wishing to leave rural China be put off by the disaster described in Figure 6.20?

6 Population

What is migration?

Migration and resources

Throughout history large numbers of people have migrated to find a better way of life by exploiting the earth's natural resources. One of the most famous of these mass migrations happened just over 100 years ago in the USA. It is a good example of the hardships people will put up with in search of resources and money.

▽ Figure 6.23

The Californian Gold Rush

During the summer of 1848, the news that gold had been found in California spread up and down the West Coast of the USA and across the border to Mexico. Newspapers were full of stories of men who claimed to have become rich overnight by mining gold in California. That winter, people from all walks of life set out for California. Many sold all their possessions to get there. The gold seekers, also known as Forty-Niners, joined the rush from as far off as Europe and Australia. Many Chinese also flocked to San Francisco to join in the gold rush.

By far the greatest number of Forty-Niners walked or rode across the American continent to reach the Gold Fields of California. Some used the Oregon trails over the Great Plains where the spring rains made some of the trails almost impassable. The rains were followed by an epidemic of cholera, which killed thousands of the travellers. Nevertheless, by 1852 more than 200 000 gold seekers had managed to reach California.

△ Figure 6.24 Direction of the Gold Rush

△ Figure 6.25 A Gold Rush town

ICT links

To find out more about the Californian Gold Rush, its effects on people and the environment, take Oakland Museum's virtual tour:

http://www.museumca.org/goldrush/

Activities

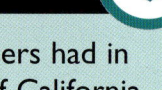

1. Make a list of the problems the Forty-Niners had in their great migration to the Gold Fields of California.

2. When they got to the 'Gold Towns' they lived very hard lives. Imagine you are one of these Forty-Niners. You share a cold, damp room with 10 other people.

You have very little money, but you still believe that you will strike it lucky and find gold. Write a letter home to your sisters telling them of your journey and your life in Two Horse Creek where you live. Use information from the website opposite to help you.

Many people migrate because they simply do not have a choice. They are forced to move away from their homes, villages and communities. There can be many reasons for this including wars or natural disasters, but just like the gold rush, the attraction of natural resources is a cause of many forced migrations.

❯ The Narmada River Project

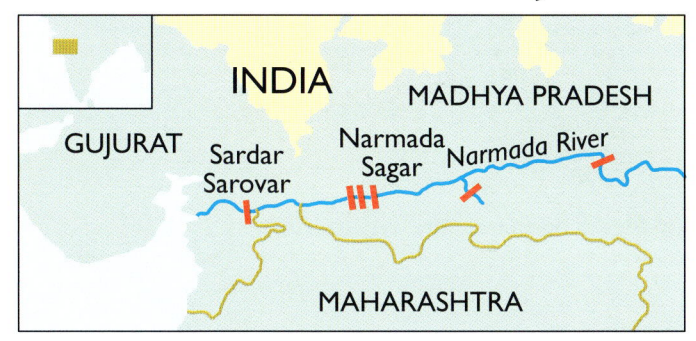

Figure 6.26 Map showing dams on the Narmada River, India

The example we will use is the Narmada River Project, India. The natural resource, unlike gold, is much easier to find but just as precious to people. It is water!

The Indian Government:
- Realises the growing population of the country needs feeding.
- Needs to make more electricity for growing industry.
- Wants international help with the project.

The Narmada Bachao Andolan (Save the Narmada Movement), which is spearheading the protest, says the project will displace more than 200 000 people apart from damaging the fragile ecology of the region.

NBA activists say the dams will submerge forest farmland, disrupt downstream fisheries and create flooding that will increase the risk of insect-borne diseases. Some scientists have added to the debate saying the construction of large dams could cause earthquakes. But those in favour of the project say that the project will supply water to 30 million people and irrigate crops to feed another 20 million people.

Figure 6.27 Sardar Sarovar dam, Narmada River project

FACT FILE: NARMADA

Project began in 1979

3 200 dams to be built along 1 200km Narmada river

Gujarat, Madhya Pradesh, Maharashtra and Rajasthan likely to benefit

Opponents says it will displace 200 000 people and damage ecology

World Bank withdrew in 1993

To be fully complete by 2025

Activities

3 Use the map, Figure 6.26, to describe the locations of the main dams in the project along the Narmada.

4 What 'population pressure' is India facing for the government to create this project?

5 Make a list of all the positive and negative things that can come from the project.

6 Use the following headings to classify your ideas:
- Environment
- Economy
- Society

7 What is your opinion? Explain whether you think the project is a good or bad thing.

6 Population 119

Assessment tasks

Background

In this chapter you have covered all the main ideas about population. Now you will use what you have learnt to complete an investigation into the environmental impacts of people using the natural resources of Nigeria: oil and gas. Over these pages there is information about the population of Nigeria and the oil company, Shell Nigeria.

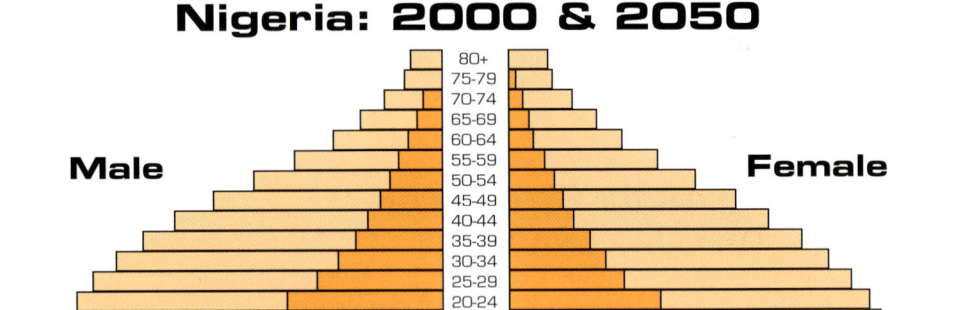

FACT FILE: NIGERIA

Nigeria is located on the West Coast of Africa and came into being in 1914

It covers a land area of 923 768.64 square km

The climate is sub-tropical

The population growth rate is around 3% per year

The capital city is Abuja

Nigeria gained independence on 1 October 1960

The official language is English

Nigeria changed from a military regime to a democratic civilian government on 29 May 1999 with the swearing in of President Olusegun Obasanjo

△ **Figure 6.28** Nigeria: Key Facts

△ **Figure 6.29** Predicted population change in Nigeria: 2000 to 2050

The population pyramid for Nigeria shows both the figures for the years 2000 and 2050. From it you should be able to see how the population of the country is likely to change in this time. But how will this have an impact on the country's economy and the quality of life for the people of Nigeria?

▽ **Figure 6.30** The location of Nigeria

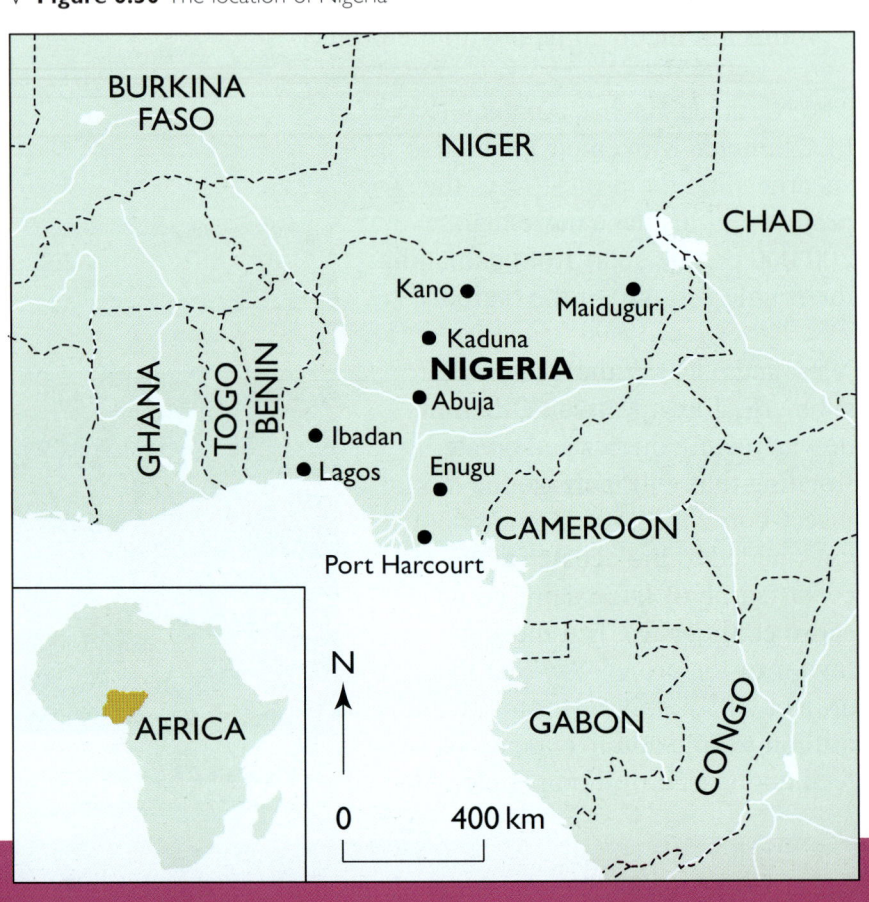

120 INVESTIGATING GEOGRAPHY A

Shell's operations are based in the Niger Delta and the nearby shallow off-shore area. The Delta covers an area of 70 000 square kilometres, making it one of the largest wetlands in the world, with the world's third largest mangrove forest. The population of the Niger Delta is about 7 million people, and is growing at about 3% a year. The region holds some of the world's largest oil reserves.

Activities are concentrated on land, swamp and shallow offshore areas. Production comes from 94 oilfields across the Niger Delta that use over 6 000 km of pipelines. The Nigerian economy is dependent on the oil sector which provides half of the country's GDP, but only a small percentage of the workforce. Still over half of the population work in agriculture, many on small **subsistence farms**.

▽ **Figure 6.33** From Shell Nigeria website

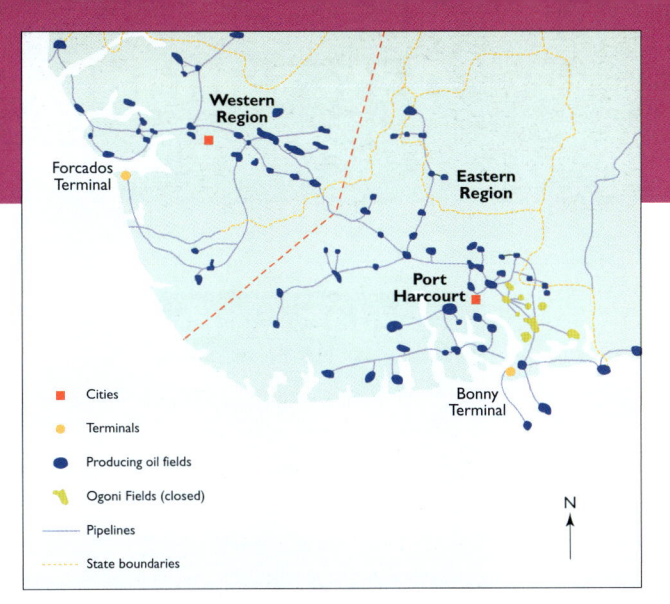

△ **Figure 6.31** Shell's operations in the Niger Delta

△ **Figure 6.32** Drilling for oil in the Niger Delta

Major Oil Spill at Yorla Well-10

Incident

A major oil spill has occurred at Yorla Well-10 in the Ogoni area. The spill was first reported late on Sunday 29th April, 2001 by a local community leader. A preliminary helicopter survey the following morning found that a mixture of oil and gas was spraying from the well head. The well location within the nearby forests was just over one kilometre from the nearest community.

Evidence provided by the well-control experts showed that the incident was caused by sabotage, that is, the deliberate damage of the well-head by unknown persons to create a leak.

Immediate actions taken

- Shell Nigeria immediately set up a dedicated emergency response team to deal with the incident.
- The appropriate local, state and environmental authorities were notified of the incident.
- Shell Nigeria brought in well-control experts from the US to help in bringing the well under control.
- Shell Nigeria also notified the neighbouring Ogoni communities and sought their co-operation to help get equipment into the area to stop and contain the spill.
- Emergency relief supplies of food and water were arranged for communities nearest to the spill site.
- A mobile clinic was stationed in the area to attend to any medical emergencies.

△ **Figure 6.34** Environmental problems related to the oil industry

The most common environmental problems related to the oil industry are: oil spills, gas flaring, dredging of canals and land taken for the construction of facilities. Shell Nigeria's policy is that all activities are planned and executed to minimise environmental impact.

6 Population 121

Assessment tasks

Target tasks

1 Read pages 120–21. Then, write a report about the advantages and disadvantages of the oil industry for Nigeria. Use the questions in Figure 6.35 to help you structure your report. You can add extra points. Use facts and figures to back up your ideas.

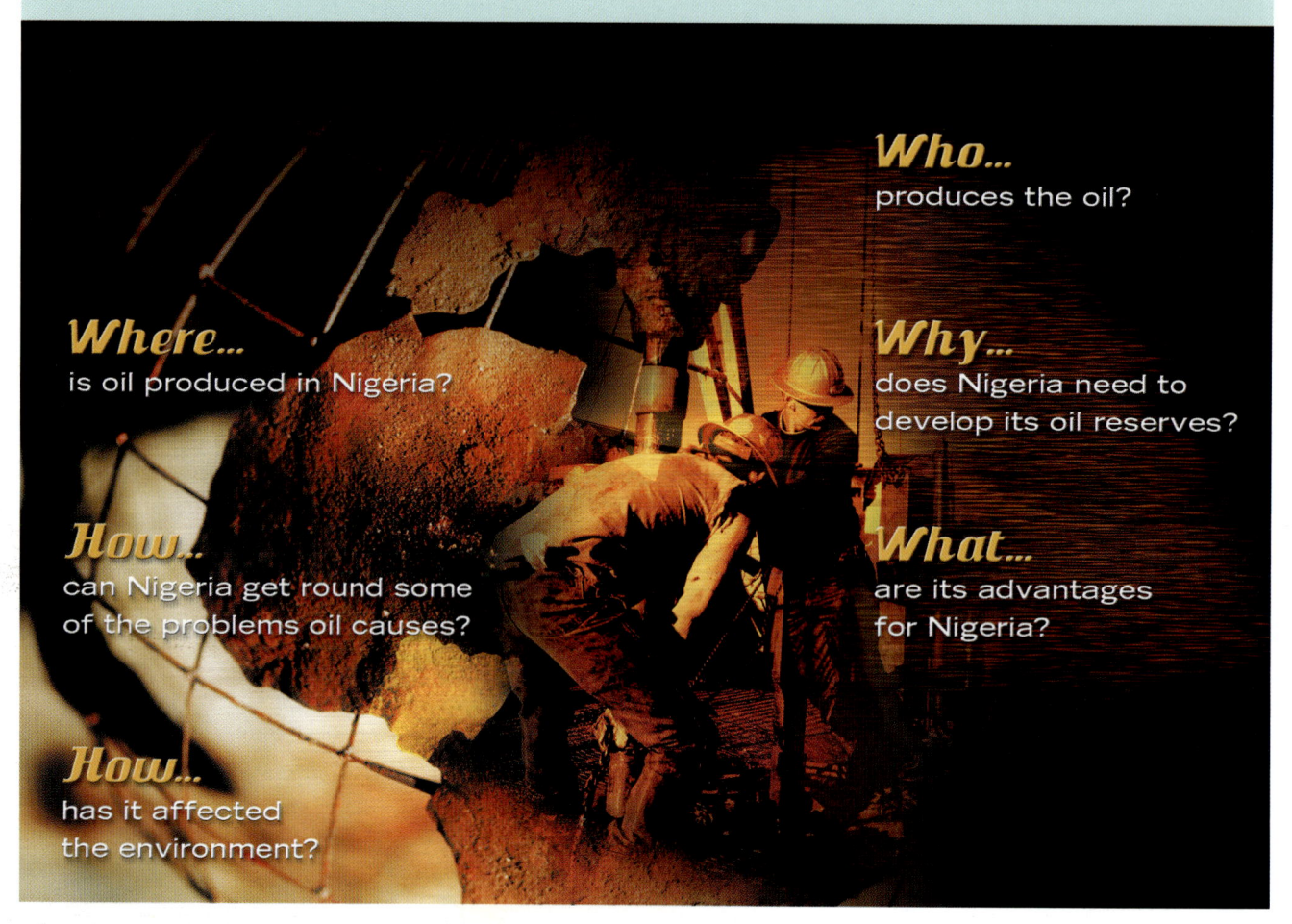

Where... is oil produced in Nigeria?

How... can Nigeria get round some of the problems oil causes?

How... has it affected the environment?

Who... produces the oil?

Why... does Nigeria need to develop its oil reserves?

What... are its advantages for Nigeria?

△ Figure 6.35

Extension tasks

2 Read pages 120–21. Then, write an account with the title 'What are the advantages and disadvantages of the oil industry for Nigeria?' Use the questions suggested in Figure 6.35 but think of at least one more for each list yourself. Put your answers to the questions in a logical order. Structure your report in sections. Use facts and figures to back up your ideas.

ICT links

General statistics:
www.your-nation.com

Population pyramids:
www.census.gov/ipc/www/idbpyr.thml

Review

At the beginning of this chapter we said that you would study theory, patterns and processes connected with the topic of population. Now it's time to review what you have done.

People live in different places for different reasons. Some crowd together in large settlements, while others live far away from big groups. As populations develop they change their birth and death rates often because of the level of economic development in the country. We monitor the structure of countries' populations through population pyramids.

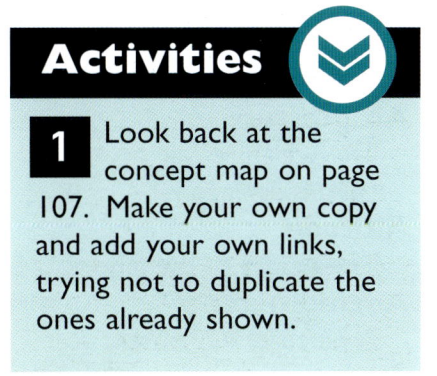

Migration of people can be caused by many factors, both voluntary and involuntary. It has an impact on the receiving country and the one losing people.

People will always try to exploit an area's natural resources to their advantage. It is only in the last few years that people have realised the importance of protecting the environment from these activities.

Activities

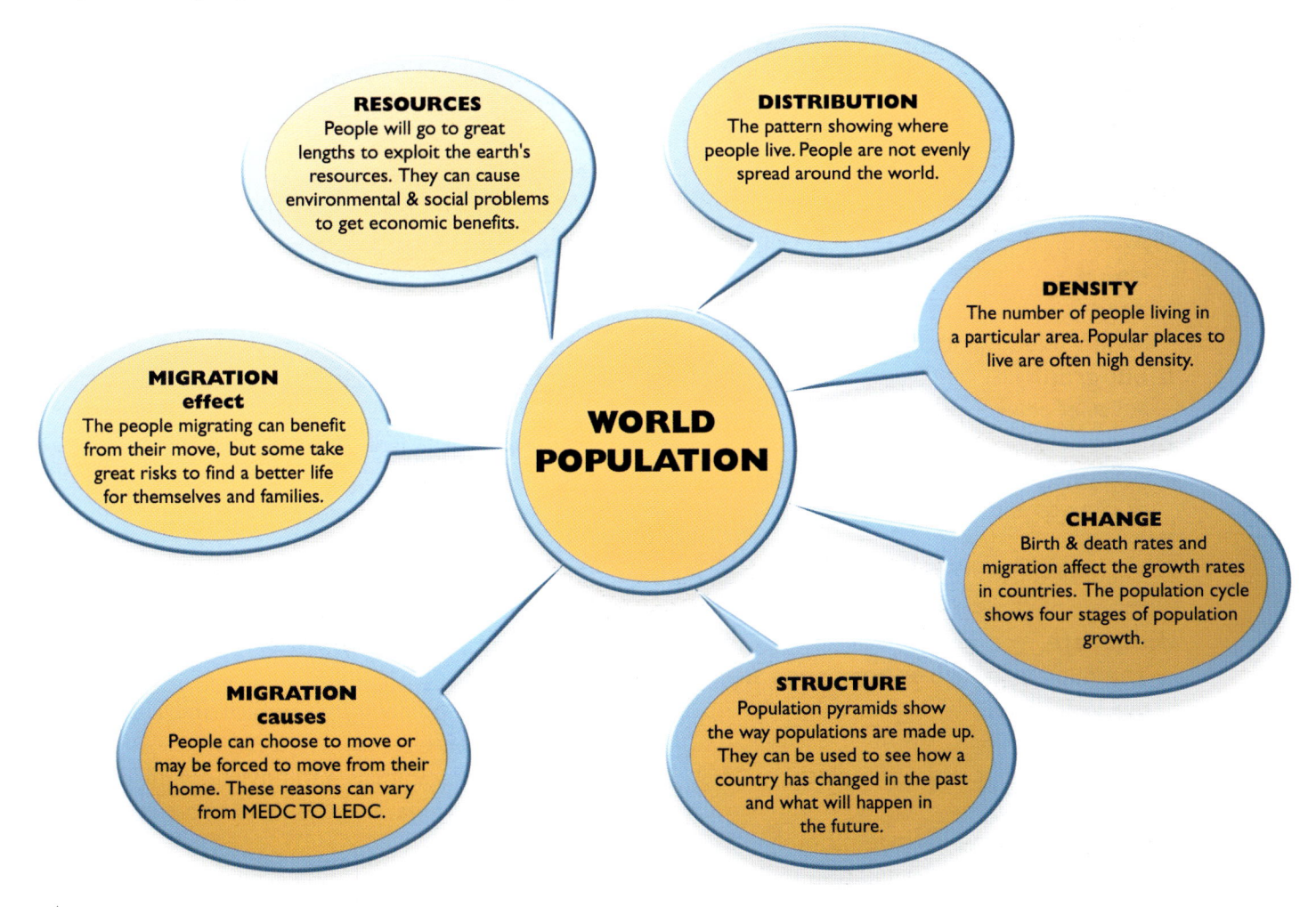

1 Look back at the concept map on page 107. Make your own copy and add your own links, trying not to duplicate the ones already shown.

WORLD POPULATION

- **RESOURCES** — People will go to great lengths to exploit the earth's resources. They can cause environmental & social problems to get economic benefits.
- **DISTRIBUTION** — The pattern showing where people live. People are not evenly spread around the world.
- **DENSITY** — The number of people living in a particular area. Popular places to live are often high density.
- **CHANGE** — Birth & death rates and migration affect the growth rates in countries. The population cycle shows four stages of population growth.
- **STRUCTURE** — Population pyramids show the way populations are made up. They can be used to see how a country has changed in the past and what will happen in the future.
- **MIGRATION causes** — People can choose to move or may be forced to move from their home. These reasons can vary from MEDC TO LEDC.
- **MIGRATION effect** — The people migrating can benefit from their move, but some take great risks to find a better life for themselves and families.

△ **Figure 6.36** Population: a summary

6 Population 123

Glossary

Accessibility
How easy a place is to get to.
Air pressure
The weight of air pressing down on the earth's surface.
Altitude
The height of the land above sea level.
Anemometer
A piece of equipment to measure wind speed.
Area
An amount of land.
Atmosphere
The layer of gases around the Earth.
Automatic weather station
Equipment linked to a computer to record the weather.
Barometer
A piece of equipment used to measure air pressure.
Beaufort wind scale
A number scale used to identify different wind speeds.
Bedouins
A group of nomadic people who live in the desert.
Biased
A one-sided point of view.
Bibliography
A list of reference sources.
Biome
A large-scale ecosystem with the same type of climate and vegetation.
Biomass
The amount of living material in a particular area.
Birth rate
The number of babies born per 1 000 people per year.
Climate
The average weather of a place.
Climate graph
A graph to show average monthly temperature and precipitation for a place.

Community
A group of people, plants or animals having something(s) in common.
Compare
How things are the same or different.
Conflict
Where the interests of one or more groups clash.
Congestion
An unusually high build up of something, e.g. traffic, people.
Continent
The largest unit of land the earth is divided into.
Contrast
How things are different.
Convectional rain
Rain caused by warm air rising.
Death rate
The number of deaths per 1 000 people per year.
Demographic transition
A graph showing a model of the changes in a country's birth and death rates.
Derelict
Land which has fallen into disrepair.
Desert
An area which receives very little rain.
Distance
How far it is from one place to another.
Distribution
The spread of something, e.g. population, across an area.
Eastings
Grid lines on an OS map that run from top to bottom of the map.
Economy
An area's or country's wealth and resources.
Ecosystem
The plants, animals and environment of a particular area, and the links between them.
Emigration
People moving out of a country.

Environment
 The total features – living and non-living – that make up a place.
Environmental decay
 A decline in the quality of the surroundings for people, plants or animals.
Equator
 Latitude 0 degrees – an imaginary line which divides the earth into the northern and southern hemispheres.
Evaporated
 A liquid which has been turned into a vapour.
Field sketch
 A sketch drawn outside the classroom looking at a real landscape.
Fieldwork
 Finding out about a place by visiting it.
Finite
 A limited resource, one that will run out, e.g. oil.
Flash floods
 A flood that happens quickly and without warning.
Fossil fuels
 Sources of energy formed from the remains of animal and vegetable matter, e.g. oil and coal.
Front
 Where cold and warm air meet.
Frontal rain
 Rain caused by warm air rising up over cold air and condensing.
Geographical enquiry
 A sequence of geographical questions.
Global Positioning System
 The use of satellites and receivers to locate places.
Global warming
 The rise in the temperature of the earth's atmosphere.
Globe
 A round shape that represents the earth.

Greenwich meridian
 Longitude 0 degrees.
Grid reference
 A way of using numbers or letters to locate places on maps.
Hemisphere
 A half of the globe.
Honeypot site
 A popular tourist location which attracts many visitors.
Human geography
 Features that have been built by people.
Humidity
 The quantity of water vapour held in the air.
Immigration
 People moving into a country.
Industrial inertia
 The tendency for an industry to remain in a particular place even though the original reasons for that choice are no longer as important.
Informal economy
 Casual, irregular work, e.g. street-selling.
International
 From places in other countries.
Isobars
 Imaginary lines joining up places with the same air pressure.
Land use
 What people build on and do with the land.
Landscape
 What an area of land looks like.
Latitude
 Numbered lines on the globe that are parallel to each other from east to west.
Latitude
 The angle of a place from the centre of the earth, e.g. the North Pole is 90 degrees north.
LEDCs
 Less Economically Developed Countries: the poorer countries of mainly South America, Africa and Asia.

Line drawing
A simple sketch with lines and some labels and notes.

Local area
The area within a few kilometres of where you live.

Location
The place where something is found.

Longitude
Numbered lines on the globe that run from the North Pole to the South Pole.

Map projection
How a map is drawn so that a curved surface can be shown on a flat sheet of paper.

Maritime
Influenced by the sea.

MEDCs
More Economically Developed Countries: the richer countries of mainly North America and Europe.

Meteorologist
A person who studies the weather.

Microclimates
The climate of a small area caused by local factors.

Migration
People moving from one place to live in another.

Minimum–Maximum thermometer
A piece of weather equipment which can measure the highest and lowest temperatures in 24 hours.

National
To do with a country.

National Park
An area of outstanding natural beauty, protected by law and managed by Park authorities to conserve the environment for future generations.

Neighbourhood
A district where people live.

Nomads
People who live in mainly desert areas but are not permanently settled in one place.

Non-renewable resource
One that will run out because there is a limited amount of it, e.g. oil.

Northings
Lines on an OS map that cross from side to side.

Ordnance Survey
The organisation responsible for drawing the main maps of the UK.

Pedestrian
Travelling on foot.

Physical geography
The natural features of a place, such as hills.

Population cycle
see **demographic transition**

Population density
The number of people living in a given area.

Population distribution
The pattern of where people live.

Population growth rate
The amount a country's population increases each year.

Population pyramid
A graph showing the structure of a country's population.

Population structure
The way a country's population is split between males and females of different ages.

Precipitation
Water which falls from the sky in liquid or solid form, e.g. rain, hail, sleet, snow.

Prevailing wind
The most common direction the wind blows from.

Primary industry
Extracting raw materials from the land or sea.

Primary sources of evidence
First-hand evidence, e.g. data from fieldwork.

Public park
A recreation area in a settlement.

Pull factors
The things which attract someone to migrate to a place.
Push factors
The things which force someone out of a place.
Quaternary industry
Managing information and/or using information technology.
Rain gauge
A piece of weather equipment to measure the amount of rainfall.
Redevelopment
Redesigning and/or rebuilding an area.
Reforestation
Replanting an area with trees.
Regenerate
Bringing a run-down area back to life, improving it.
Regional
A large area that, in the UK, consists of several counties.
Relief rain
Rain caused by air being forced to move over upland areas, e.g. hills.
Renewable resource
One that will not run out, e.g. the wind.
Representative fraction
A way to write the scale of a map, e.g. 1:50 000.
Reservoir
A purpose-built lake to store water.
Reunification
To join again, e.g. East and West Germany rejoining.
Rural
To do with the countryside.
Sahel
A band of semi-desert, which runs east to west, to the south of the Sahara.
Scale
The amount by which real places are reduced so that a map can be drawn.

Sea currents
Layers of warm and cold water moving through the sea.
Secondary industry
Processing raw materials into manufactured products.
Secondary sources
Information from books, maps, the World Wide Web, etc.
Services
Facilities, e.g. shops that people can use.
Skidoo
A cross between a motorbike and water ski that can be used on snow.
Stevenson screen
A box used to hold and protect weather equipment.
Subsistence farming
Growing food mainly for the family to eat.
Synoptic chart
A map of weather recorded at individual weather stations.
Synoptic code
Symbols used to show the weather recorded at weather stations.
Temperate maritime climate
A mild climate, influenced by the sea.
Temperature range
The difference between the hottest and coldest temperatures over a period of time.
Tenement blocks
A large building divided into a lot of different homes.
Tertiary industry
Providing a service either for an individual customer or a company.
Theme park
A recreation area which has rides and other attractions.
Thermometer
A piece of weather equipment used to measure the temperature.

Traditional industries
Primary or secondary industries that use old methods.

Transnational company
A large company operating in more than one country.

Tube wells
Long hollow holes to allow people to get water from deep below the soil.

Urban
A built-up area, e.g. a city.

Venn diagram
A diagram showing relationship by overlapping circles.

Vertical air photo
A photograph taken looking directly down on the land.

Vocational
Related to a particular type of work.

Weather
The day-to-day changes in the atmosphere.

Wind rose
A diagram used to plot wind direction.

Wind vane
A piece of weather equipment to find the direction of the wind.

World Heritage sites
Through the United Nations, internationally agreed sites of historic, wildlife, cultural and natural value.

Glossary 129

Index

accessibility 74, 124
Africa 76, 120–2
air pollution 15
air pressure 52, 124
Alaska 19, 94
Algerian climate 60, 61
altitude 59, 124
anemometers 48, 124
area 124
atmosphere 45, 124
automatic weather stations 124

Bangkok 56
Bangladesh 76, 78
barometers 48, 124
bears 96, 97
Beaufort wind scale 52, 124
Bedouins 124
biased information 18, 124
bibliographies 19, 124
biomass 124
biomes 62, 124
Birmingham 61
birth rates 110, 111, 112, 123, 124
Brazil 78
Bristol 8, 9

Cairo 56
Calcutta 56
Californian Gold Rush 118
Californian National Parks and sites 94, 95–7
Castleton 89, 90, 91, 92, 93, 99
Catlin, George 94
Chesterfield Football Club 74, 75–6
China 70, 71, 78, 117
choices 27, 28
climate 45, 54–63, 124
climate graphs 54–6, 61, 124
clothing industry 76–7
coalfield areas 69
community 38, 124
comparing places 16, 124
conflict 96, 97, 100–2, 124
congestion 124

continent 124
continental climate 60
contrasting places 16, 124
convectional rainfall 59, 60, 124

death rates 110, 111, 112, 123, 124
demographic transition 112–13, 124
derelict land 72, 124
deserts 55, 60, 124
development 24–43
digital photos 11
distance 124
distribution 124
Dover 116, 117

Eastings 6, 124
economic activity 64–83, 90, 91
economy 38, 124
ecosystems 100, 124
Eden Centre, Cornwall 62
emigration 114, 124
entrepreneurs 125
environment 9, 125
environmental decay 34, 36, 125
Equator 12, 13, 125
Ethiopia 110, 111
European Pilot Fund 34
evaporation 60, 125

field sketches 11, 125
fieldwork 17, 125
finite 125
flash floods 60, 125
fossil fuels 125
France 110, 111
frontal rainfall 59, 125
fronts (weather) 59, 125
futures frame 41, 42

genetically modified 125
geographical enquiry 17, 125
Germany 24, 25, 26, 27, 28, 31, 38–9, 40, 42
Ghana 24, 25, 26, 27, 28, 30, 31, 32, 36–7, 40, 42, 43
Gladstone Pottery Museum 34, 35

130 INVESTIGATING GEOGRAPHY A

global links 14–15
Global Positioning System (GPS) 4–5, 12, 125
global warming 125
globe 12–13, 125
Greenwich meridian 12, 13, 125
grid references 6, 125

Hawaii 94
hemisphere 125
Hetch Hetchy Valley 96
Hollins Cross 91
honeypot sites 89, 125
human geography 8, 9, 108, 125
humidity 125

immigration 114, 125
India 119
Indonesia 76, 78
industrial inertia 74, 125
industrial location 74, 126
informal economy 66, 125
information, checking on 18–19
international 125
International Meteorological Organisation (IMO) 49
Internet 14
isobars 125
Istanbul 56

Japan 70, 76
Johannesburg 56

land use 8, 9, 125
landscape 34, 125
latitude 4, 12–13, 59, 125

LEDCs (Less Economically Developed Countries) 66, 67, 70, 71, 76, 77, 79, 114, 126
Lima 56
line drawings 11, 126
local areas 10, 27, 126
location of industry 74, 126
London 10, 16, 63
longitude 4, 12–13, 126
Lower Don Valley, Sheffield 72, 80–2
Lulworth Cove, Dorset 11

Luton airport 15
Lyn River (Dorset) 16

map projection 12, 126
maps 6, 7, 8, 9, 50–1, 54, 90, 91
maritime climate 60, 126
MEDCs (More Economically Developed Countries) 66, 71, 77, 114, 126
Melbourne 56
memory maps 24, 43
Meteorological Office 49
meteorologists 47, 126
microclimates 58, 126
migration 107, 114–19, 123, 126
mind maps 24, 43, 86
minimum–maximum thermometers 48, 126

Namibia 55
Narmada River Project 119
national 126
National Parks 17, 84–103, 126
natural resources 107, 123
neighbourhoods 38, 126
New York 94
Nigeria 120–2
nomads 46, 126
non-renewable resources 126
Nordbad project, Dresden 38–9, 40, 42
Norilsk, Russia 63
Northings 6, 126
Northumberland Coast 99
Obuasi gold mine, Ghana 36–7, 40, 42, 43
oil industry 120–2
Ordnance Survey (OS) 126
   - maps 6, 7, 8, 9, 90, 91

Peak District National Park 89–93, 99
pedestrian access 38, 126
physical geography 8, 9, 108, 126
pollution 76
population cycle see demographic transition
population density 28, 107, 109, 123, 126
population distribution 107, 109, 123, 126
population growth rate 107, 110, 120, 126
population pyramids 111, 120, 122, 123, 126
population structure 107, 111, 123, 126

Portinatx, Ibiza 18
precipitation 45, 126
prevailing winds 59, 60, 126
primary industries 66, 69, 126
primary sources of evidence 17, 126
public parks 86–7, 127
pull factors in migration 114, 125, 127
push factors in migration 114, 115, 127

quality of life 27, 28, 29, 41
quaternary industries 66, 127

rain gauges 48, 127
rainfall 55, 63
recycling 33
redevelopment 34, 127
reforestation 127
regeneration 127
regional 127
relief rainfall 59, 127
renewable resources 127
report writing 20, 22
representative fraction (RF) 7, 127
reservoirs 96, 127
reunification of Germany 38, 127
Rio de Janeiro 56
Romania 78
rural areas 8, 58, 127
sahel 127
San Francisco 56
satellites 5
scale 30, 127
sea currents 127
secondary industries 66, 69, 127
secondary sources 17, 127
services 127
Sheffield steel 70, 72, 73, 74, 80
Shell 120–2
Shipping Forecast 52, 53
sketching a scene 11
skidoo 127
South Korea 70, 71
Sri Venkatasvara 64
statistics 10
steel production 70–2, 73, 74
Stevenson screens 48, 127

Stoke-on-Trent potteries 26, 27, 32, 34–5, 40, 41
subsistence farming 121, 127
synoptic chart 127
synoptic code 50–1, 127

temperate maritime climates 60, 127
temperature range 55, 127
tenement blocks 38, 127
tertiary industries 66, 69, 127
textile production 76–7
Thames, river 16
theme parks 127
thermometers 48, 126, 128
traditional industries 34, 128
transnational companies (TNCs) 78–9, 128
tube wells 36, 128

UK climate 59, 60
UK employment structure 68
United States (USA) 70, 94–7
urban areas 8, 58, 128

values and geography 27, 30, 41
Vancouver 56
Venn diagrams 33, 128
vertical air photos 8, 9, 128
vocational training 38, 128

weather 44–53, 128
West Africa 76, 120–2
wind rose diagrams 53, 128
wind speeds 63
wind vanes 48, 128
World Heritage sites 95, 98–9, 128
World Meteorological Organisation (WMO) 49
World Wide Web 17, 19
writing about a place 10

Yellowstone National Park 94
Yosemite National Park 94, 95–7
young people's concerns for the future 28–9